HOW TO GET RICH ON OTHER PEOPLE'S MONEY

HOW TO ORDER:

Quantity discounts are available from Prima Publishing & Communications, Post Office Box 1260HC, Rocklin, CA 95677; telephone (916) 624-5718. On your letterhead include information concerning the intended use of the books and the number of books you wish to purchase.

U.S. Bookstores and Libraries: Please submit all orders to St. Martin's Press, 175 Fifth Avenue, New York, NY 10010; telephone (212) 674-5151.

HOW TO GET RICH ON OTHER PEOPLE'S MONEY

Going From Flat Broke
To Great Wealth
With Creative Financing

TYLER G. HICKS

Prima Publishing & Communications
P.O. Box 1260HC
Rocklin, CA 95677
(916) 624-5718

Typography by Miller Freeman Publications
Production by Bookman Productions
Jacket design by The Dunlavey Studio

Prima Publishing & Communications
Rocklin, CA

Library of Congress Cataloging-in-Publication Data

Hicks, Tyler Gregory
  How to get rich on other people's money: going from flat broke to great wealth with creative financing / Tyler G. Hicks.
    p.   cm.
  Includes index.
  ISBN 0-914629-61-1: $17.95
  1. Success in business.   I. Title.
HF5386.H4852   1988   87-31867
650.1—dc19   CIP

88 89 90 91   RRD   10 9 8 7 6 5 4 3 2 1

Printed in the United States of America

WHAT THIS BOOK DOES FOR YOU

Making a fortune today is different from five years ago, ten years ago, twenty years ago. Why? For a number of reasons, namely:

- *People are different today.* There are millions of young men and women who never served a day in the military, never had trouble finding a job, never were laid off from work. So they see life differently from those born earlier.
- *People expect fast results.* Instead of filling out a coupon and addressing an envelope, finding a stamp and walking to the local mailbox (if one can be found), people want to call a toll-free 800 number and have their purchases delivered the next day by Express Mail or by one of the overnight delivery services.
- *People don't want to wait a lifetime* to "make it"—they want it *now,* not tomorrow, not next year! *Now,* today, here! Using *no* money of their own!

This book shows *you* how to get rich today, meeting all the above criteria. It gives you sure-fire "electronic" techniques to build riches quickly and with certainty using Other People's Money—OPM, I call it. With this book *you* will:

- Be able to get hard cash in just days.
- Make money from today's needs without a rented office.

- Make the whole world your golden oyster of riches.
- Get filthy rich in the best tax haven ever created.
- Flood your life with wealth from creative financing.
- Make a fortune walking (or jogging) along Easy Street.
- Get money that need never be repaid—money without strings.
- Strike it rich using small seeds to grow big fortunes.
- Rake in unlimited gold from the salt of the earth.
- Laugh *all* the way to the bank using wild, workable ideas!

Every method in this book is practical—it *does* work because one or more of my millions of readers has used it to build wealth *today!* Toss away your musty, soggy, wealth-building books of yesteryear. You're at the close of the twentieth century when things, and people, *are* different!

Today, everyone wants "real-time" results when they make efforts to build a fortune. While you can still build wealth working from your kitchen table, you can't get rich fast selling items priced at $1. A price of $100—or more—is what's needed today. In this book I show you how I've sold millions of dollars worth of items from my basement ping-pong table! (My wife wouldn't let me work on the kitchen table.)

Need money for your business or real estate deals? I've helped people raise millions in their spare time. And I show *you* how to raise the business or real estate money you need, quickly and easily! No need to sweat it out scratching around for funds. Use today's methods to get money from modern lenders and you'll get all the money you need, with creative financing methods!

Make the world your golden oyster. Do business anywhere and make big profits at it. In this book I show you the how, and where, of making a big fortune from worldwide trade. Easily, quickly, using FAX, Telex, letters of credit, and low-cost couriers.

Want to shelter the money you make? I give you the greatest tax haven ever created! See your profits on your computer CRT, if you wish. Figure your low, low taxes using fast, accurate software. Or get an accountant to do this for you on another computer. But above all, walk away with a big bundle of cash in your pocket to buy videotapes to watch on your VCR at your leisure.

Want to be flooded with really *big* money, millions and up? Then come with me while I show you how to latch onto the megabucks! Many of my readers have done just that, today. And they winter in the Virgin Islands, swimming off their palatial yachts when they feel like it. You, I'm convinced, can do the same.

The best street to walk, in my opinion, is Easy Street. And I show *you* how to take a stroll on this street. Or you can jog it, if you wish! And while getting all this great exercise, you can be making money! Could anything be more attractive? Build muscle tone while increasing your bank account with creative financing.

Free money *is* available these days! And in greater amounts than ever before in history. *You* can make some of this money yours, using the space-age tips in this book. Take giant shortcuts to surefire money—without strings!

From small seeds grow giant fortunes. Learn how to:

- Get really big money for good ideas.
- Never have to repay any of this money.
- Receive cash infusions if you need more money.

So stop scratching around for cash! Get *all* the money you need in this age of information and desktop publishing.

Convert the salt of the earth—real estate—to gold! Come with me as I show how my readers and I have:

- Built holdings of many millions on *zero* cash.
- Had a *positive* cash flow since day one.
- Sold properties at big profits in a short time.

Your fortune today can come from the fast-food generation (reared by a TV babysitter) that's looking for a place to live!

You *can* laugh all the way to the bank. My readers and I do it almost every day of the year! While our ideas may be termed "wild," they really aren't! They're just unusual uses of standard banking methods. Such ideas even turn bankers on.

Why? The ideas are so much in keeping with banking practices, that bankers say, "Why didn't I think of that?" You, who *did* think of it, can laugh as you deposit big checks.

Yes, making money *is* different today, in many, many ways. For instance, we no longer have "mail order" or "direct mail." Today we have "direct response." And we have "marketing warfare" and "guerilla marketing tactics." All these terms, and many more, reflect the changes in the marketplace.

You *can* get in on the money-making methods that prevail today. Just turn to Chapter 1 and we'll start on the road to making *you* rich! Today. Not ten years from now, but today, here and now.

Along the way, you'll learn how I'm always here day or night to answer your questions, help you get loans, even lend money on good business deals (or real estate). I'm no more than a quick phone call away.

Let's start making *you* rich now, using OPM—Other People's Money! I'll show *you* how to go from flat broke to great wealth with creative financing using other people's money. So let's start getting you rich!

TYLER G. HICKS

CONTENTS

CHAPTER 4

GET GLORIOUSLY RICH IN THE BEST TAX HAVEN EVER

CHAPTER 5

HOW TO BE FLOODED WITH CASH TO BUILD WEALTH

CHAPTER 6

MAKE A FORTUNE WALKING (OR JOGGING) EASY STREET   98

CHAPTER 7

USE A GOLDEN TOUCH TO GET MONEY WITHOUT STRINGS   117

CHAPTER 1

HOW AND WHERE TO GET FAST, HARD CASH, NOW

Do you need fast, hard cash for a business or real estate investment? If you do, there are millions of dollars available to you today. Quickly, easily—without yards and yards of red tape!

How can I say this? I can say it because for the last thirty years I've helped Beginning Wealth Builders (*BWBs* I call them) raise millions of dollars for all kinds of business and real estate deals. During that same time I've been (and still am) President and Chairman of the Board of a lending group with assets of more than $100 million. So I speak from long— and highly successful—experience in getting money for BWBs.

Understanding the Borrowing Process

In years of encouraging people to borrow money to build a fortune, I've tried to explain to them the borrowing process. Just so you're on the same "wave length" that I am, Figure 1.1 illustrates the way the borrowing process works for my friends. (All the people who I help are my friends—you have a friend in Ty Hicks. Remember that!)

As you see in Figure 1.1, the lender puts money into *your* hands in the form of a loan. You use this money to buy or start a business or real estate venture. This venture earns money, part of which is a profit. From this profit you take a share for yourself. Part of the remaining profit you use to repay the

1

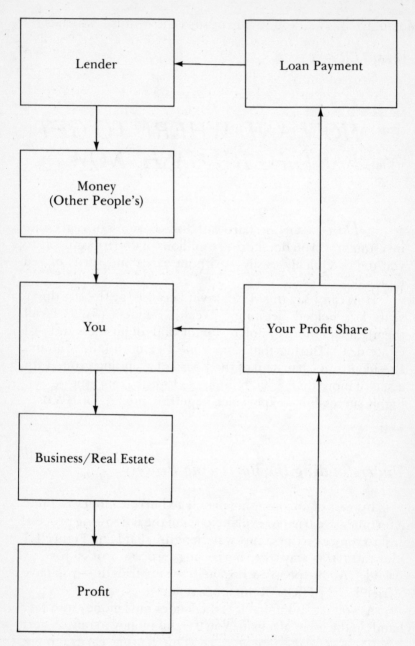

Figure 1.1 *How the Borrowing Process Works for You*

loan that allowed you to buy or start the venture, which is re-paying the loan. You're using the power of Other People's Money—OPM.

Is this magic? No! It's the way smart BWBs have built wealth for centuries. Why isn't the method better known? Because the people who use it are so busy counting their money that they don't have time to tell others about the enormous power of borrowed money to build great wealth for anyone willing to work at using it! But this book tells *you* all you need to get started.

Proof by the Thousands

My office files bulge with thousands of letters written by BWBs telling of the power of borrowed money in their business lives. (I regard real estate investments made to earn a profit as *business* investments because the purpose of any business investment is to earn money for the owners.) These thousands of letters tell of what BWBs are doing *today* to use the incredible wealth-building power of borrowed money. Here are parts of two recent letters. Read them with the open mind all BWBs have. And know that *you* can do the same—or better!

Thanks for the inspiration your books have provided me in my development as a real estate investment entrepreneur. To this day, when I feel overwhelmed by demands of property management and development, I refer to the commentaries and passages in your books to recapture the spirit and zeal they evoke inside me.

I am very proud and happy to report that my property holdings now produce sufficient cash flow to live on comfortably. I am therefore leaving my banking career as an assistant vice president to pursue property purchase and management on a full-time basis. Specializing in three- and five-family buildings, here's an approximate income statement:

	BLDG. 1	BLDG. 2
Rent	$20,500*	$44,300
Expenses	−6,000	−5,500
Mortgage payments	−10,750	−19,800
Net profit	$ 3,750	$19,000

	BLDG. 3	BLDG. 4
Rent	$44,500	$41,800
Expenses	−8,000	−7,500
Mortgage payments	−19,500	−18,500
Net profit	$17,000	$15,800

*My family and I occupy one apartment rent-free

* * * * *

Recently I read your book *How to Make One Million Dollars in Real Estate Starting With No Cash.* I began buying real estate one year ago when I was twenty-one and had no credit. Now I have a lovely home, two co-op apartments, a five-family and a six-family, all for *no down payment.* They appraise for just under $800,000. It still amazes me that I own real estate.

There you have two BWBs building their wealth *today.* Not ten years ago, not even five years ago. But today!

And *you* can do the same—*today!* Using borrowed money—fast hard cash I call it. I'm so certain that you *can* do what these BWBs are doing that I stand ready to help you, as a friend, day or night. So let's get you a loan—*now!*

Loans by the Dozen—Take Your Pick

Some of the most creative business people in the world work for lenders. Why do I say this? Because today's lenders are constantly coming up with new ways to get people to borrow their money.

And why do lenders spend sleepless nights trying to find new ways to entice customers to borrow? Because the competition between lenders is so intense that the only way to survive is to come up with new ways to "throw money into people's faces." Other people's money!

For example, my financial institution is—as we say—so liquid (money on hand) that we slosh! What does this mean? It means that we—like many other lenders today—have more cash on hand than we can find borrowers for. So we have to spend much of our time looking for qualified "takers" who will borrow our money.

To show you a few of the ways lenders use to get people to borrow their money, the following are some recent ad headlines advertising money available for business and/or real estate deals:

- No Income-Verification Loans.
- Fast-Turnaround Fixed-Rate Mortgages.
- Private Mortgage Money Available.
- 100% Insider Financing.
- How to Take the Hassle Out of Business Loans.
- Jumbo Money Available—Now.
- Need Commercial Financing Fast?
- Cash-Out Refinancing.

I could go on and on with other interesting headlines designed to get a borrower to take the lender's money. So if you're thinking, "Oh, I can't qualify for a loan, my credit is no good," stop right now. There *are* plenty of lenders who say:

- Bad Credit? *NO* Problem!
- Bankruptcy—*NO* Problem.
- No Income Check, Ever.
- No Job Verification Needed.

Yes, there *are* dozens of new offers from lenders every week. And there are thousands of lenders just waiting to make you that loan you need. The keys to getting that loan are so simple that anyone can use them. And I mean *you!*

Keys to Getting Your Loan Quickly

Many BWBs don't think through their loan needs before applying and find that getting a loan takes longer than planned. You can cut such delays by using the following keys to getting any business or real estate loan:

1. *Apply to the right type of lender.* Some BWBs apply for a real estate loan at a business lender's office. They don't get a loan because the lender makes only other kinds of loans. So know your lender first!
2. *Seek a loan in the lender's range.* Some lenders won't lend more than $500,000; others won't lend less than $500,000. So be sure the amount of money you're seeking is within the lender's range.
3. *Type your loan application.* Don't submit a handwritten loan application for a business or real estate loan. It will almost never be approved. Typing is the accepted means of communication in business. Use it!
4. *Don't tell the lender "Time is of the essence."* Nearly every BWB borrower thinks this sentence will produce the money tomorrow—or even today. Not so! "If time is so important," thinks the lender, "why did the borrower wait this long to apply? Can't the borrower plan his or her time better?"
5. *Don't "bug" the lender with constant phone calls asking when you'll get your money.* The lender is likely to say "Never!" just to get rid of you. Wait for the lender to evaluate your application and give you an answer.
6. *Keep "hunger" out of the application.* Sure, you may be on your last legs, the sheriff may be knocking on the door, your kids may have to wear hand-me-downs, and you don't know where your next meal is coming from. But do *not* let this show in your application! Lenders turn away from hungry borrowers because such borrowers frighten them. Be relaxed, cool, competent, polite—and you'll get a loan.

Although you may not agree with the above keys, let me say they *do* work! And that—to me—is the measure of any method. Does it work? Some of my readers happily report:

Tell Ty Hicks his methods of borrowing really work. Using his borrowing techniques, and starting with nothing, I now have an $80,000 a year business. That's my first year's gross!

* * * * *

I have been reading and studying your books for some time. I opened accounts at four different banks and applied for a loan at each. So far I received $10,000 in loans. All are nonsecured personal signature loans.

Be Ready to Get Your Loan

You can use a loan to do many things that will zoom your wealth. For example, you can:

- Buy a going business.
- Start a new business.
- Expand an existing business.
- Save a nearly failed business.

A loan gives you great power to build your future wealth. Knowing this, you should take every positive step you can to get the loan you need.

To be ready to get the loan you want, see the loan from the lender's view. In my lending activities where we're lending some $25 million or more each year, we look for three characteristics in each loan deal. These are the "go signals" we and all other lenders look for:

- *Capacity* is your ability to repay the loan on the terms acceptable to yourself and your lender. This means that if you agreed to repay the loan at the rate of $1000 per month for seven years that you *can* meet these payments without too much stress on your budget. So be sure to indicate in your loan application that you *will* have a large enough cash flow from your business or salary, or both, to make the agreed-on periodic repayments on your loan.
- *Collateral* is hard assets your lender can attach if you can't repay your loan. Because a lender uses profits from his or her business to make a loan to you, the lender wants to be certain the loan will be repaid. Why? Because each dollar of profit represents many hours of work. If any of these dollars are lost because you can't, or won't, repay the loan, the lender is hurt badly. But if there's some type of collateral (for example, real estate, machinery, stocks, bonds) that the lender can take over, it's a lot easier to make the loan. And remember, good friend, a cosigner with a steady income is good collateral!
- *Character* covers your desire and intention to repay the lender. Though it may surprise you, there are some people who take out loans with little intention of repay-

ing in a timely manner. To show a possible lender that you have a strong desire and intention to repay the loan on time, include in your application or cover letter a budget listing showing the monthly loan payment and how it will be made each month until the loan is repaid in full.

So, good friend, if you should come to me for a business or real estate loan, your chances for a *"YES"* answer are excellent if:

- Your loan application is typewritten.
- We make the type of loan you're looking for.
- The amount of your loan is in our range.
- You're willing to give me a few days to answer you.
- You have the ability to repay the loan.
- You have suitable collateral to pledge.
- You show me in a letter that you *will* repay us.

Now that you have some idea of how to impress any lender favorably, let's take a look at the many ways for you to get money *today*. And be sure to remember that I am here to help you every step of the way! Stick with me, and you'll build a fortune on other people's money.

Use the Power of the Printed Word

Some of you who've read some of my earlier books know that I publish a monthly newsletter—*International Wealth Success*—which gives many details and tips on borrowing money. Each month my newsletter lists dozens of lenders seeking borrowers. And each month there are dozens of people who run free ads looking for money. And, as one reader told me on the phone: "My ads really got results for me. I found a lender for my $50,000 loan. Ty, I'm on my way!" You'll find full information on the newsletter on page 32 of this book.

You can advertise for lenders. Believe it or not, lenders *do* read ads run by people seeking business or real estate loans. In advertising for a loan, you're using the power of the printed word. And believe me, good friend, the power of the printed word is beyond belief! I'm the author of over seventy pub-

lished books, and people keep writing me—day and night—
for help.

What kind of an ad might you run to get a loan? That's
easy. Just sit down with pencil and paper and write out what
you need. Here are a few examples of ads that pull well for
BWBs:

- LOAN NEEDED to buy successful auto-repair business. Monthly repayment will return your $35,000
  loan in three years with 12% interest. Call 123–4567.
- $50,000 LOAN NEEDED to start wedding-dress busi-
  ness. Collateral available. Call 123–4567.
- I NEED $250,000 to expand my growing business.
  Great collateral offered. Call 123–4567.

What if you don't have any collateral, may have a "slow-
pay" credit history, or may have gone bankrupt in the past?
You're—as we say—a "worst case" situation. (Please don't
be offended—I'm just trying to paint the worst possible picture to show how you can still get a loan.) If you have any or all
of these conditions, you need help.

Help from a *cosigner, comaker,* or *guarantor.* Each does the
same job—helping you get your loan—but in a different
way. Thus,

- A *cosigner* agrees to repay your loan in the event you
  are unable or unwilling to do so.
- A *comaker* is really a coborrower. That is, the comaker
  is equally liable to repay the loan.
- A *guarantor* guarantees that the loan will be repaid.
  But a guarantor is *not* a borrower as a comaker is. Instead, the guarantor pledges some collateral or asset
  that assures the lender the loan will be repaid.

For most BWBs, getting a cosigner is the fastest and easiest way to get a loan if their credit isn't the strongest. To get a
cosigner, use the power of the printed word:

- COSIGNER NEEDED for $50,000 business loan. Will
  pay liberal fee to cosigner after loan is obtained. Call
  123–4567.
- CAN SHOW BIG PROFIT on $100,000 business loan.
  Will share with cosigner who helps get loan. Call
  123–4567.

How much will you have to pay a cosigner, comaker, or guarantor? That depends on with whom you're dealing. But the top fee is a *one-time* amount of 5 percent of the loan *after* you obtain the money—*not* before. *Never pay front money of any kind for a loan.* You *can* get OPM without paying front money!

As the amount of your loan increases, the fee percentage decreases. Thus, on a $1 million loan the fee might be 2.5 percent, *after* you get the loan. Again, note that this is a one-time fee—not an annual fee.

You can use the power of the printed word even further by joining the Global Cosigner and Money Finder Association. This organization, described on page 197, publicizes your need for a cosigner under a code number so your identity is kept confidential. Although no organization can guarantee to find a cosigner, GCMFA does *guarantee* to circulate your need widely.

And if you're a do-it-yourselfer, you may want to get the "Guaranteed Loan Money Kit" (page 201). It gives you specific detailed, step-by-step instructions on finding cosigners, comakers, and guarantors for loans. We don't have space here to duplicate all the great and tested ideas in that kit.

When looking for cosigners, take time to prepare a simple list of all your relatives, friends, business associates, and/ or friends of friends and business associates who might cosign.

Although none of these may cosign for you, some might recommend people who *will* cosign. Because the exercise won't cost you anything except some time, it's really worth trying. Why don't you start right now, right here? Fill in as many lines as you can on a sheet of paper—the longer the better!

Put Your Telephone to Work

There are thousands of lenders around the world who make loans by phone. While the actual loan doesn't go through phone wires, the information needed for the loan and a temporary approval does. What's more, many of these lenders have an 800 phone number. This means your long-distance calls to these lenders are free!

How do loans by phone work? They depend on the following information:

- Type of loan you seek.
- Amount of money you need.
- Length of time for which you need the money.
- Your income and expenses.

Many lenders making loans by phone will overlook a poor job or business history, bankruptcy, or other financial problems if you own your own home and have some equity in it.

In helping BWBs get loans by phone, I tell them that with just thirty-two words and fifteen seconds of time they can get a *"Yes"* or *"No"* answer from a lender. So you really need not put too much time into finding out if you can get a loan for your deal.

And—if you want—you can become a Loan-By-Phone Broker to help others get loans this way. You'll earn a good commission on each loan you place. Of course, if you place a loan for yourself, you'll have to skip the commission. You can get full information on being a Loan-By-Phone Broker from the kit of the same name (page 200).

Make the Mail Bring Your Money

Some people don't like to use the phone. While I really can't understand this view because I'm on the phone day and night helping readers of my newsletter, I respect people's views. So I say, use the next best way—the United States Postal Service—the best in the world! You *can* get loans by mail—it's done every day of the week. And the money you get by mail is just as good and just as powerful as the money you get in a bank or from another lender.

To get loans by mail, you take these easy steps:

- Get the names and addresses of mail-order lenders.
- Find out what kinds of loans they make.
- Tailor your loan application to meet their requirements.

- Fill out the lender's loan application.
- Send the application in by mail.
- Watch the mail for a response.

Most mail-order lenders will get you your answer in seven days or less. In my lending organization we try to give the borrower an answer in twenty-four hours. Sometimes it takes us less time; once in awhile, it's a bit longer—thirty-six hours. But at least 95 percent of our borrowers get their money within twenty-four hours after their loan applications are approved. We call it the fastest OPM around!

So don't look on mail-order loans as slow because they take longer than loans by phone. I tell our borrowers, "Any loan money is welcome! Because you didn't have to work for loan money, you save enormous amounts of time and energy. This helps you reach your financial and life goals much faster."

You can become an expert in mail-order loans by using the Loans-By-Mail Success Kit, described on page 200. It helps *you* get your mail-order loan. And it also shows you how to help others—for a nice commission—get loans by mail. You really should have this kit if you want to get lots of loans by mail.

Get Credit Card Loans Fast

Today we all live in a world of instant gratification: People don't want to wait weeks and weeks to get something they need. You'll find plenty of people getting money they need for business or real estate by using the credit lines on their credit cards. Although the interest rate may be higher than with a signature loan, the money you get from a credit card loan is just as useful and powerful as any other borrowed money. You can put it to work quickly and easily.

Most credit cards offer a line of credit allowing you to write checks up to a certain amount, say $5000. So you just use these checks to invest in the business or real estate that interests you. And the interesting aspect of credit cards is:

- Credit card issuers don't care how many cards you own.
- Issuers' views are the more cards, the better!

- You can have a line of credit on each card without other issuers caring.

You can become—as some have—a "plastic million-
aire" with your credit cards! Just multiply the number of cards
you have by your line of credit on each (if it's the same), and
you may be a millionaire! Thus, just 200 credit cards (not a
very large number these days), each with a $5000 line of cred-
it, will make you a "plastic millionaire" (200 × $5000 =
$1,000,000).

To get a credit card you must apply for it. If you've been
bankrupt or a very slow payer of your bills, you may find it
hard to get your first card. Not to worry, as the British say.
There are ways to get that credit card, which is the first of
many. Here's how to do it:

1. Apply for a *secured credit card* at a bank that issues
   such cards.
2. *Deposit enough* in a savings account to get your credit
   card. This is usually $300 or $500, though you can, if
   you wish, deposit more if you have it.
3. *Use your credit card* to make a purchase as soon as you
   get the card. Why? Because it gets you into the credit
   stream of the world.
4. *Pay your bill* for the purchase *as soon as it comes in.*
   Don't wait even a day. Establish a "quick-pay" reputation. This will save you on interest cost and make you
   a "thirty-day wonder"—one of those people who pay
   in thirty days or less.

Most banks issuing secured credit cards will allow you to
use one-half of the amount you have on deposit for charges on
your card. Thus:

AMOUNT ON DEPOSIT	YOUR USABLE CREDIT
$300.00	$150.00
500.00	250.00
750.00	375.00
1000.00	500.00

Once you've had your secured card for a few months and
have made some timely payments on your charges, your bank
will probably increase the amount of usable credit you have
from one-half to three-quarters.

will probably increase the amount of usable credit you have from one-half to three-quarters.

AMOUNT ON DEPOSIT	YOUR USABLE CREDIT
$300.00	$225.00
500.00	375.00
750.00	562.00
1000.00	750.00

After a year or so of timely payments on your card, you may find that your bank removes the deposit requirement on your card and allows a modest line of credit. Thus, you may get a line of credit of $500, plus freedom from any deposit requirement.

Again, *use your card immediately.* Then, *make your payments as soon as you receive your bill.* Your credit report will improve, and you'll have more money. And, best of all, other card issuers will be after *you* to accept and use their credit cards!

Once you have a card with one bank that's *unsecured*— that is, doesn't need a backup deposit—you'll be swamped with offers of other cards. And by keeping your credit clean by making timely payments on every credit card bill, you can become a credit card millionaire! On OPM, yet.

One of the best sources of information on banks issuing credit cards and their specific requirements, is Louis Gorchoff's excellent book *Money Raiser's Directory of Bank Credit Card Programs.* You'll find full details of this book on page 197.

Use the "Reverse Flip" Method

When you use the money you borrow to buy something of value, you might wish to consider using a "reverse flip" to reward your cosigner or guarantor. With a reverse flip, you assign to your cosigner or guarantor the item (such as real estate or machinery) you bought. Then, any payments you make on the item will be credited to your cosigner or guarantor when (and if) the item you bought reverts to him or her because you stopped making payments on the loan you used to buy the item.

By assigning to your cosigner the item you buy, you prove several important points to him or her:

- *You are sincere* in your efforts to build wealth; otherwise you wouldn't assign the asset.
- *Much of the risk for the cosigner is removed.* Most assets go *up* in value while you're paying off the loan; your cosigner or guarantor is protected by the asset's value increase and the paydown on the loan.
- *Your willingness* to let the full asset go back to (called *revert to*) the cosigner or guarantor shows your intense desire to protect your helper while building wealth for yourself.

You will, of course, pay a nominal fee to your cosigner or guarantor for his or her help. If you don't have the money for the fee, you can offer a percentage of the income from the business, or a percentage of the profit you realize on the sale of the business, or a combination of the two. With any of these plans, you avoid an immediate outlay of money for the fee.

As an example of how your cosigner or guarantor might profit from a percentage of the gain when the business is sold, here's a recent letter:

> I bought *How to Borrow Your Way to a Great Fortune,* believed it, went out and borrowed $10,000, and bought a business brokerage. Never in my life had I sold anything; by profession I'm a dental technician. But reading your book and following the instructions made me make a decision, and today I'm doing good. I was recently offered $25,000 for half my brokerage.

So consider the reverse flip. It may be just the answer *you* need to get the loan that will build *your* riches quickly!

Aim for "Big" Signature Loans

People call me on my business phone day and night (8:30 AM to 4:00 PM and 8:00 AM to 10:00 PM EST) to tell me about the great deals they're swinging. Some talk about really big financing—"$10B"; that's ten *billion* dollars. And just recently they've started talking "10T"—ten *trillion* dollars!

My answer to all these dreamers is, "We're just small potatoes back east here. But we have Wall Street and the Statue of Liberty, plus a few other attractions. If you're interested in a signature loan up to $50,000, we'll be delighted to talk. But the Bs and Ts are out of our world!"

Some, the smart ones, listen. The dreamers, however, go off on their own, chasing the Bs and Ts. The smart ones often wind up with a "big" signature loan.

And what do I mean by a big signature loan? By big I mean: A big signature loan is any loan you get by simply signing an application and a promissory note for an amount of $35,000 or more. No collateral is pledged for the loan.

Now I know the people looking for the Bs and Ts won't think a $35,000 loan is big. Yet the lenders who are making such loans (banks and finance companies) *do* think that a $35,000 *unsecured* loan *is* big. Why? To free up $35,000 in funds for just *one* loan, the lender must do at least $350,000 in business, if the lender has an after-tax profit of 10 percent. Because $350,000 in business means lots of work, hours, and risk overcome, the lender is extremely cautious about making the loan. Remember: A signature loan means that all the lender has as collateral is some ink on a piece of paper! A lot less ink than in a new ball-point pen.

Yet, big signature loans *are* available. Just check with your commercial bank. One well-known bank currently makes personal loans up to $35,000 on the following:

- Secured *only* by your signature.
- In the form of a line of credit that doesn't cost a penny until you start using it.
- With your money just a phone call away once your line of credit is approved.
- With your check mailed to you the same day you request it on the phone.
- And *no* personal interviews are needed; you can fill out the application in the privacy of your own home, at your leisure.

Other lenders offer more flexible terms on their big signature loans. For instance, a lender that goes to $20,000 on such personal loans

- Has fixed or variable interest rates.
- Offers flexible monthly repayments.
- Lends for a variety of purposes—repairs, vacation, travel, education, or business, for example.
- Gives a 3 percent cash refund on the interest, *after* you repay the loan in full.
- Has *no* hidden charges (for example, fees, points, or prepayment penalty) of any kind.
- Provides fast loan service with an 800 number for toll-free calls to the lender.

Although these "big" loans using a signature as collateral may not seem large to some people, others put them to effective and profitable use. An example is from this BWB who writes,

> I read several of your books and used many of your ideas to improve my financial status. In the last year I bought two eight-unit apartment buildings at a time when I had *no* money. I used 100 percent borrowed money. In just one year I increased my net worth from $8,000 to $50,000.

So don't scoff at these "small" loans! They can make *you* rich. Start getting your personal signature loan at your local commercial bank. Just drop in, give them a call, or write a short note. Then you may write me a letter telling me how successful you've been! Getting OPM for yourself—fast.

Explore Credit Union Loans

There are some 20,000 federal credit unions in the United States today, plus thousands of state-chartered credit unions. These lending institutions are giving the banks plenty of competition in the areas of personal, business, and real estate loans. You should check credit unions in your area to see

1. If you're eligible to join.
2. What types of loans they're making.
3. How large a loan you might get.

Some credit unions limit their membership to employees of one company. Other credit unions are associated with religious groups, fraternal organizations, governments, and the like. If you can't qualify with any such background, consider a "central" credit union—that is, one that's open to any and all residents of a state or city. To find such a credit union in your area, just check your local "Yellow Pages" under the heading "Credit Unions." You can join a credit union free of charge and can get many benefits including

- High-interest savings accounts and Certificates of Deposit.
- Low-interest loans for many purposes.
- Kind, attentive, understanding service.
- Fast loan approval.
- Long repayment period.
- No points, fees, or other charges.

To get a loan from your credit union, take these easy, fast steps:

1. Find out what types of loans they like.
2. Get a copy of the loan application(s) used.
3. Fill out the application for your loan, *typing* it throughout.
4. Comply with *all* the credit union's regulations.
5. Submit your application; wait for an answer.

Most credit unions today are interested in making good loans, so you'll find the welcome mat is out for you. To ensure getting the loan you seek, remember to

- *Be professional* in all your dealings; this will win respect and loan approval.
- *Stand out above the crowd* by typing your loan application and meeting *all* the rules of the credit union's committee.
- *Never threaten* or otherwise try to force the credit union into doing what you want. Instead, do what the credit union asks; you'll get many more loans that way!

Remember that credit unions *want* to make loans. Why? Because their whole objective is to help people improve their financial condition. Don't turn away from a credit union loan—it could be the answer to *your* wealth-building start!

See if an Annuity Would Work for Your Loan

Life insurance companies, along with real estate lenders, are among the most creative firms around. Their recently introduced "whole-life annuity" might get you the loan you seek. There are other names for this type of annuity. But they all get the same results, namely:

- *The annuity acts as collateral* for a loan you get from a lender other than the insurance company.
- *It grows in amount* for seven or ten years until the annuity equals the amount you borrowed.
- *The lender is ensured* that the principal (the amount you borrowed) will be repaid whether you live, die, or fail to repay the loan.

To buy such an annuity, the borrower must put up about one-third of the amount of money borrowed. Some borrowers try to borrow the cost of the annuity, giving them the loan free and clear. This *can* work; the only tough part is finding a lender who will finance the annuity. Although this is possible, it usually takes a little longer than finding a direct lender for a project.

To see how an annuity works—in very brief detail and without the many legal wheres and wherefores—let's take a $100,000 ten-year loan as an example:

> Amount of annuity at full value = $100,000
> Loan amount needed = $100,000
> Cost of annuity today = $33,300
> Length of annuity = Ten years
> Net to you if annuity is taken out of loan =
> $100,000 − $33,300 = $66,700
> Net to insurance company = $33,300

There *are* lenders who will advance money to you with an annuity as their collateral. The best way to find such lenders is to read my book *Business Capital Sources,* described on page

194. Or, you can look in the "Yellow Pages" of your phone book under "Loans," "Banks," or "Finance."

You *can* get the borrowed money you need. And that money can grow in the form of an investment you make. One reader writes,

> I started using your techniques and built $2000 of borrowed money into $120,000 net worth in just two years. I have a real estate firm, a trout farm, and a sports store.

So ask your insurance broker about a single-premium life annuity. Then study the information carefully. It just may give you the loan you seek.

Look for Over-Appraised Assets

When you go out to buy an asset such as an income producing building, a cargo airplane, or a printing press, it usually will be appraised by a professional. This person will say in a written report that "This asset is worth $300,000 in today's market."

Now, when you want to buy that asset using OPM, a lender will usually loan 75 percent of the appraised value. So on the $300,000 asset mentioned above you could borrow $0.75 \times \$300,000 = \$225,000$ on a long-term loan — defined as twelve years or longer. The balance, $\$300,000 - \$225,000 = \$75,000$, would have to come from your savings or from another loan.

But what would happen if the seller were willing to sell this asset for $225,000? Then you'd be able to get the asset with *zero* cash. This is called 100 percent financing and is an excellent example of using OPM to build your wealth. Why might someone be willing to sell an asset at less than the appraised price? There are any number of reasons, such as:

- A strong desire to unload a burdensome asset.
- An asset is owned by an estate that wants quick cash.
- Family problems make the seller want a quick sale.
- The owner "wants out" so badly any price is acceptable.

Although you may not have run into such reasons yet, I assure you that they occur every day, somewhere. How do I know? Because my reading public keeps me informed through visits, phone calls, and letters as to what they're doing *now,* today. These readers wrote,

> In the last six months I bought $500,000 worth of income real estate with *no* money down. Each of these properties gives me a positive cash flow, every month! Now I'm looking for more real estate to expand my holdings and income.
>
> * * * * *
>
> I took over three buildings for no money down. One is an office building; the other two are rental homes.

So be on the lookout for over appraisals. They could be your source of great wealth on OPM.

Apply at Many Different Lenders

You *can* get more than one loan at a time. This can give you multiples of OPM. At my lending institution we have plenty of people with two, three, and even four loans—all at the same time. Thus, a person might have a long-term mortgage for, say, $475,000, an auto loan for $20,000, and a signature loan for $5000.

And do you know what? We're *happy* this person took all these loans from us. Why? Because if he or she didn't take them from us, I'm sure they would have gone elsewhere. So we'd have lost the business—namely the interest income we earn on each of these good, solid loans.

And I'm also willing to bet you—though I haven't checked the actual record—that this person has other loans with other lenders. Just as long as the payments can be made in a timely fashion, we lenders are happy!

I've urged BWBs for years to use OPM in the form of multiple loans. Why? Because with multiple loans,

- Each loan is smaller, meaning that it's easier to get the money.

- The more loans you get, the more money you'll have to build your business wealth.
- Having several loans will make you a more ambitious business person—you have to be, if you wish to pay your loans off!
- Managing the payments on several loans at once will train you to be a much better manager.

Readers *do* build wealth using multiple loans. They write me nearly *every* day of the year telling me how multiple loans *are* working for them. This reader from the state of Washington wrote,

> I followed your advice in your book and applied at seven different lenders for a $6000 signature loan from each lender. Five said "Yes," and I got $30,000. I used this money as the down payment on a video rental store, which is doing $120,000 a year with a net of about $24,000 a year after paying my wife's salary (she runs the store). Thanks so much for your methods, which really work!
>
> *   *   *   *   *
>
> I read your book *How to Borrow Your Way to a Great Fortune* about three and one-half years ago. I put some of your principles to work and have gone from a net worth of $12,000 to a net worth of over $333,000.
>
> *   *   *   *   *
>
> I bought my present business, a tavern, using the Ty Hicks method. I took out three loans of $5000 each and have since paid back one-third of each. Or, I should say my business paid them back and will continue to do so. I also took out an auto loan, which my business pays back, too. My business also pays all notes ($47,000 per year). The three loans above were for the $10,000 down payment and other fees (legal, inventory, and so on). My net—after the business pays all bills and loans—is about $800 a week; this gives me about $40,000 per year. But when all notes are paid off, I'll have another $47,000 a year income!

There you have three modern-day proofs that multiple loans *do* work. And they *can* work for you! Just convince yourself—if I haven't already done so—that OPM:

- Can be the most powerful force in your business life.
- Offers you salvation from a dull, dead-end job with surly, unappreciative bosses.
- Gives you the opportunity to build a fortune, even if you don't have a spare thin dime to your name at this time.

When I started looking for work as a teenager, my family was so poor they couldn't afford to have my shoes resoled. So I cut out pieces of newspaper and put them in the bottom of my shoes so my socks wouldn't touch the ground. But in the rain and snow, the water soaked through the paper making my feet freeze. Yet by using the power of OPM, I was able to rise above such humble beginnings; today I loan my excess money to BWBs so they won't have to stuff newspapers in their shoes to plug the holes.

And I've heard the stories of all the doomers and gloomers who say it can't be done. It *can* be done! It *is* being done! And you—I'm convinced—*can* get multiple loans today, just as the above BWBs did.

Sure, it's true that your credit will be checked by most lenders. But you can get around poor credit as I showed you earlier in this chapter. And some lenders may not even bother to check your credit if you show them that you're a sincere, hard-working borrower who *will* repay the loan.

To get multiple loans quickly and easily, take these steps:

1. *Decide* what types of lenders with whom you want to work (banks, finance companies, mortgage brokers, savings and loan associations, and credit unions).
2. *Get the names* of a number of such institutions in your area. I recommend that you work locally at first because lenders will have a greater sympathy for you and your plans.
3. *Contact each lender* by phone, by mail, or in person. Ask for several copies of their loan applications. At the same time, ask for any printed information that they have on their loans.
4. *Tailor your loan application* so it meets the interests of your target lender. Type every application as recommended earlier. Ask only for the type of loan the lender makes.

5. *Submit your application* with a brief letter telling the lender about your sincerity and your desire to repay the loan fully in a timely manner.
6. *Continue submitting applications* to other lenders, using the same procedure. Keep sending out your applications until you have submitted one to every lender on your list. *Never* give up!
7. *Wait for a response* from each lender. Don't call, asking for a response. Wait—the response will come when the lender is ready to contact you.

One last thought: If any lender asks why you sent applications to five or ten different lenders, reply in full truth: "I'm looking for the best deal. So I sent applications to all lenders who appear to be qualified to handle my needs and whose reputation is excellent."

Find Loans Close to Home

Many BWBs almost go into convulsions when I tell them they might be able to get loans nearby at 0 percent interest, 3 percent interest, or 4 percent interest. "That's impossible!" they say. "Who would give a loan at zero percent interest? I never heard of such a thing."

That's when I have to tell these "smart" BWBs that "Just because *you* never heard of something, doesn't mean it can't be! Close your mouth and start listening. You just might learn something! Remember: You ain't learning when you're talking."

You can find very low-cost loans close to home in the following places:

- Your state Job Development Agency (or an agency having this function but a different name)
- Your state business Development Agency (or an agency having this function but a different name)
- Your city Job or Business Development Agency (or an agency having these functions but different names)
- Your county Job or Business Development Agency

These agencies, which you can find in your local telephone book under the heading of "Government" (usually the blue pages), are delighted to make loans to local people to create new jobs, build factories, train workers, and expand existing businesses. Note that these are *not* personal loans. Instead, they are business or real estate loans. Such loans are made to businesses providing local jobs, real estate operations for business, training activities for local workers, and, other business or real estate use.

To encourage business and real estate people to accept this readily available money, interest rates are held *very* low. Also, rates are held low so that the company accepting the money can still earn a profit, even though they're paying off one or more business loans.

How can *you* latch onto some of these zero-interest or very low-interest funds quickly and easily? Here's what you can do:

1. *Find out* which agency in your state, city, or county makes the type of loan you need.
2. *Do this by calling* (or writing) the information office for your state, city, or county, as listed in the blue pages of your local telephone book.
3. *Ask for information* on the various loans, grants, and other forms of assistance available to you and your firm. You will be quickly sent this data free of charge because most agencies are actively seeking to make new loans, grants, or other types of advances to stimulate business and jobs.
4. *Fill out the application* or other forms required to get the funding you seek. *Be certain to type every application!* Never fill out such applications in longhand — you are almost certain to be rejected.
5. *Provide all information requested,* even if some of it seems to be unnecessary. When you're dealing with a government agency, you do as requested. If you don't, you'll find that your time is wasted because you won't get the money you seek. Government personnel have *their* way of doing things. If you go along with these ways, your chances of getting the funds you seek will be much better!

6. *Wait until you are told of the decision* of the agency—
   don't "bug" your contact for an answer. It will come
   soon enough.

Don't Overlook Industrial Development Agencies

Many cities, states, and counties have quasi-official industrial development agencies that make loans, grants, and other monetary advances to local business and real estate activities. These development agencies often have private sources of funds and may have state sources.

You can apply for money from industrial development agencies in the same way as detailed above for job and business development agencies. Just remember that all these agencies want to improve business and jobs in their area. So be certain that the funds you're seeking *do* exactly that—that is, build business and jobs locally. Then you're almost certain to get the money you seek and need!

Go to Uncle Sam—He'll Help

Many BWBs I talk to shun the Small Business Administration (SBA) of our federal government saying, "Those loans take too long." Yet I have letters in my files saying, "We took your advice and went to the SBA. The money was in our hands in sixty-five days." While that may seem like a long time to some people, I've known others who waited eighty days, ninety days, and longer for a business loan from a conventional source such as a bank or commercial finance company.

The SBA doesn't always *make* loans these days. More often SBA will *guarantee* a loan. This speeds the entire process and gets you your money sooner. Additionally, you can get an SBA loan faster if you have someone ready to buy the guaranteed portion of your loan. Further, many lenders, such as my financial organization, who want greater security in the loans they make, will gladly buy the guaranteed portion of an SBA loan because it is guaranteed by the full faith and credit of the United States government.

To get an SBA loan for your business or the real estate related to your business, take these steps:

1. *Call the local SBA office* in your area. It is listed in the blue pages in your local phone book under United States Government.
2. *Ask for a business loan application.* You will be sent this completely free of charge along with information on the loans the SBA is currently making or guaranteeing.
3. *Fill out the loan application* completely, typing every entry. Be certain to answer *all* questions. Where a question does not apply to your business, mark it "Not Applicable."
4. *Send the application to the SBA,* including a letter explaining any points needing extra information. If you know someone interested in buying the guaranteed portion of the loan, include this information in your letter. It is *not* necessary to give the name of the person who will buy the guaranteed portion of your loan.
5. *Wait for a reply.* These days it should come quickly under the revamped SBA procedures. I hope you get a "Yes" response!

To understand how the SBA guarantee works, let's say that you need a $200,000 loan for business. After you send your application to SBA, you get a response stating that SBA will guarantee your $200,000 loan from a local SBA-approved lender such as a bank. You take the following steps:

1. *You apply for a $200,000 loan* at your local bank, presenting your loan approval and guarantee offer.
2. *The bank, after reviewing your application,* approves your $200,000 loan and advances this amount of money to you.
3. *Of the $200,000,* 90 percent of it, or $0.9 \times \$200,000 = \$180,000$ is guaranteed by the United States government. Thus, the bank is "at risk" for just $\$200,000 - \$180,000 = \$20,000$. And because you'll be repaying principal and interest monthly on this loan, the $20,000 will soon be repaid.
4. *The bank turns around and "sells"* the guaranteed $180,000 of your loan to someone like myself. Then

    the bank has its $180,000 back, which it can lend out to other borrowers, while still collecting on your loan.

5. *Meanwhile, a buyer like myself* gets monthly payments from the bank at an interest rate higher than I could get elsewhere. And if the borrower fails to repay the loan in full, the United States Government will make good any missing money within sixty days after the borrower's default (failure to repay). Besides, I have the fun of knowing that I'm helping a small business and the government make our great capitalistic system work better! To me, I might as well put my money to such use instead of letting it sit idly in some bank or money market account earning pennies in interest.

    The key to an SBA loan is a well-prepared application for a business that's useful to the economy. And if you can find a loan buyer, your chances of getting the loan you seek are much improved.

Don't Forget the "Little FHA"

    Another branch of our great government, the Farmers Home Administration (often called the "little FHA"), makes many loans outside agricultural business. You might be able to obtain such a loan if you have a business that will help people in a farming area. These loans are in good U.S. dollars and are just as powerful as any other type of loan.

    Because the Farmers Home Administration (FmHA) is less well known than the SBA, it is often easier to obtain a loan from FmHA. You must, of course, qualify for the loan, and it must meet FmHA requirements. To get the latest requirements and loan ranges, call FmHA in your area. Or write them if you prefer. Again, FmHA is listed in the blue pages of your local phone book. Follow the same procedure as detailed above for SBA loans, remembering that FmHA works in agricultural areas instead of general business areas.

Get Your Loan Now

There *is* money—millions and millions of dollars—available for you in the form of many different types of loans. And this money—OPM—is very powerful because it can help you

- Save time in starting or buying a business.
- Get you instant recognition by sellers.
- Give you negotiating power you don't have when money is scarce.
- Put you on the road to wealth quickly and easily.

As I said earlier, thousands of my readers write me and tell me what they've done. This reader wrote,

> I'm so glad I bought your book. It must have been destiny that I chose this one. Your instructions alone helped my partner acquire a line of credit of $10,000 from a bank that turned him down two weeks earlier.

To show readers the power of borrowed money, I've loaned them thousands of dollars through my company, IWS, Inc. And in the more than twenty years I've been making these loans, *every* reader has repaid in full! The reason why these reader–borrowers repaid in full is because the money they borrowed was so powerful they were able to pay off their loans out of their business or real estate profits.

You now know more about borrowing than when you started this chapter. And you're ready to get your loan *now!* Follow the steps given here. Just remember to be businesslike in all dealings with lenders. Remember: You will *never* go wrong in being businesslike—it can't hurt you!

And if all else fails, remember that you have a friend in Ty Hicks. Call or write, and I'll try to help. Go get that loan *now!*

CHAPTER 2

MINTING MONEY RICHES FROM TODAY'S NEEDS

You live in a different world today from the one you lived in five years ago, ten years ago. Why do I say this? People *are* different today; needs and wants of people are changing, and speed, convenience, and ease of use are key sales points for almost every product.

You can make millions on OPM in this new world of ours! All you have to do is figure out what people want. Find or develop an item or service giving people what they want. Deliver this item or service quickly and conveniently. The result? People will "throw money at you!"

Make Money From Money

You can serve the new needs of people while being paid up front. This allows you to make money from money—even though your item or service is not money. Sound strange? It isn't! Plenty of people today are doing just this (including myself). And there's room for millions more to do the same. Here's how:

1. *Look around you*—find out what people want.
2. *Listen to people*—their conversations will often tell you what people want.
3. *Figure out a way* to deliver what people want.

4. *Get the word out* that you can deliver what people say they want.
5. *Ask for payment* with the order so you can operate on OPM.
6. *Expand your sales* by offering other related items or services to your customers.
7. *Go on to great wealth* in a short time without a big factory, office building, or equipment.

Now that you know the *how* of getting rich today, what steps will you take? It's easy to read *what* to do. "But," you say, "how do I really get started?" To help you answer that question I'll show you step by step exactly how I started and built pennies into millions in my spare time. Then I'll give you the real-life experiences of other BWBs who are doing much the same, today! Meanwhile, you'll get plenty of "rules of thumb" to help you build great wealth *your* way.

Find Out What People Want

Whether you're people-oriented or a loner, you *can* find out what people want. Here's the method that works for more BWBs, including me, better than any other:

- *Look around* for the types of people you want to serve in your business—professionals, blue-collar workers, and so on.
- *Listen to them* when they talk. *Hear* what they're saying. Jot down notes about what they say. You can do your listening in restaurants, on trains, on buses, and at home (step 2, above).
- Figure out a way to serve their needs, based on what you hear from these people.

How do I apply this idea to making millions? Here's what I do; you can do much the same: *In my travels* I talk to dozens and dozens of people, doing more *listening* than talking. And, I *make notes* of what people say as soon as I leave them. (Making notes while with people seems to upset them.) (Step 1.)

My target audience is and always has been people who want to get rich in their own businesses. So when I talk to people I talk to everyone. Why? Well, almost everyone wants to get rich. My listening shows that *people—everywhere—need money* to start their own business of any kind. *Yet these people seem helpless* when it comes to finding out where the money is and how they can get it for their business use.

Hearing this again and again led me to start my own newsletter, *International Wealth Success,* which shows people the how, where, and why of getting money for business and real estate use. In more than twenty years of publishing, this newsletter has helped thousands of people get the money they need for starting on their roads to wealth (step 3).

When I started this newsletter I had to get the word out—on almost *no* money—that it could help people (step 4). So I *told all my friends* about this great new monthly newsletter for only $24 a year (and it's still just $24 per year; see the back of this book), I *sent news releases* to various magazines and other publications to get free publicity for the new newsletter, and I *mentioned the newsletter* in my books on building wealth quickly and easily.

The results were outstanding. In a matter of months I had thousands of subscribers to this great newsletter. These people are seeking and finding in *International Wealth Success* items like

- Financing sources offering 100 percent, 110 percent, 120 percent of the money needed by BWBs.
- Compensating balance loan sources.
- New sources of real estate loans of all types.
- Part-time moneymaking ideas.
- Finder-fee listings of many types.
- Fast, easy moneymaking-wealth deals.
- Secrets that can put cash into your pocket.
- Worldwide moneymaking ideas.

The newsletter led to related books and courses. These are "eaten up" by newsletter subscribers who seek more information on specific moneymaking methods. So step 6 is fulfilled. And because subscribers pay $24 for their annual subscriptions, when they request them, step 5 is also met.

Give a Valuable Bonus to Customers

To help people decide to do business with you, offer a valuable bonus for sending money. Such a bonus might be a booklet, a business machine such as a calculator, or any other *useful* item. For example, with the *International Wealth Success* newsletter subscription, we offer these bonus items to new subscribers of one year or longer:

- Copy of a book called *Can You Afford Not to Be a Millionaire?*—a 220-page paperback
- "Mail Order Lenders List," which lists many sources of lenders who loan by mail
- *How to Borrow Your Way to Great Riches,* a twenty-four page booklet by me.
- A business and real estate loan application for people who subscribe for two years or more, allowing them to apply for a low-interest loan to my company

Crazy as it seems, some people in this millionaire-maker business of ours put more emphasis on the bonus items than on what they're buying! But what do you care—so long as they send money!

Always have your bonus item(s) of a related nature to your main product. Thus, if you're "selling money," as I do, have your bonus item in the money field. For instance, we have some products in the field of improving your credit. One of the bonus items we offer is "How to Get a Mortgage Regardless of Your Credit Rating." You can see that the bonus backs up the main products—improving your credit.

See Your Business Clearly

What business are we *really* talking about here? Its modern name is *direct marketing.* In days past, it was called mail order, then direct mail. But today it's called direct marketing because you sell directly to the person buying your product. Sometimes, the name is expanded to *direct response* because your customer responds *directly* to you. So to be right up to date, we'll use the latest term—*direct response*—from now on.

Your direct response can come from any number of sales offers you make to your prospect. These offers might be through

- A *sales letter* you send to your prospect — this is the *direct-mail* way to sell.
- A *radio commercial* on a network reaching the type of customers you seek.
- A *television "spot"* — for example, thirty seconds or sixty seconds — selling your product.
- A *telephone call* to a prospect — called *telemarketing* — to sell the hearer something beneficial.
- *Space or classified ads* in publications read by your prospects; this is the *mail-order* aspect of the direct-response effort.

You can make millions through direct response. I've done it, and I know plenty of others who've done the same. Plenty of readers of my newsletter report strong income when they promote an item by direct response. One long-time reader who uses direct response for exporting products around the world writes, "My exporting is going well. I'm exporting medical equipment, lab equipment, and food-processing equipment." And he's doing all that by the direct-mail segment of direct marketing! *You* can do much the same. And I'm here to help you — step by step. Let's see how you might get started in direct response — easily, quickly, and cheaply!

Start With Your Unique Product

Think back to the last time you bought something by direct response. You bought — I'm certain — an item or service that was different from most others you could get at the corner store. You bought something *unique!*

So, if you want to make millions in direct response of any kind, remember to start with a unique product that is not easily available locally, that is priced to earn you a profit, and that has *every* aspect of its uniqueness described in your advertising. "But," you ask, "how do I find a unique product (or service) when there are thousands (maybe millions) of people looking for just such a product?"

The best way to "find" such a unique product is to

- *Develop it yourself,* based on what you see as a need in a given market—that is, group of people.
- *Have the product developed* for you by someone in the field who knows how to come up with new or revised ideas.
- *Combine two or more* existing products or services to come up with a new one.

To get the idea for your unique product, follow the seven steps given earlier in this chapter. Just be sure that the item you come up with *is* unique. It is this uniqueness that gives you a jump on the market and puts *big* bucks in your pocket.

Certain products lend themselves more easily to uniqueness than others. For example:

- *Books* are one-of-a-kind. There's only *one Gone With the Wind.* If you want to read that story, you *must* read just *that* book! So you can come up with a unique product by writing (or having someone write) a book with a new and different approach to a common problem. See if you can provide what people want (step 2).
- *Newsletters* are published to serve a definite need that people have. While there may be two or three newsletters serving one need, each newsletter will be different because the editor is a unique person.
- *Consulting services* are unique because each reflects the experience and background of the person doing the work. Thousands of financial consultants have used our "Financial Broker-Finder-Business Broker-Consultant Kit" (see back of this book) to develop a unique service for their local area while earning a *big* income for themselves.
- *Specialized services* developed for *your* area can be unique. In big cities there are shopping, dog-walking, and wake-up services—all unique and all worth the price. If you live in a small city or in the country, I'm sure there's a service that you can develop and sell to local people.

- *Many kinds of art can be unique.* There are people who sell wild west prints by mail order. Others sell nautical prints the same way. The key, in every case, is prints not available locally. Other art forms that are unique include models of ships, trains, aircraft, or autos that appeal to people who don't have the time to build them.

Now that you know a few unique products, get a pencil and piece of paper. Draw a few lines like those below and mark the information on *your paper. Do not use this book for notes unless you own the book!*

MY UNIQUE PRODUCT-DEVELOPMENT SHEET

Product Name	Unique Features for Buyers	Suitable Selling Price
_____	_____	_____
_____	_____	_____
_____	_____	_____

To help you fill out your own sheet, I show you in Figure 2.1 how I filled out the Unique Product-Development Sheet for several items I wanted to develop. All these products reached the market and are now selling well. They're helping me build more millions of income! And I want *you* to do the same for yourself and your loved ones.

Find Unique Outlets for Your Product

You have a unique product (or service) for sale by direct response. Now you must find suitable outlets for it so the money pours into your bank!

If you can find unique outlets, you're almost certain to "have it made," as they say. What do I mean by unique outlets? I mean

- *Mailing lists* that contain names of people interested in your product; lists that have not been used often by your competition.

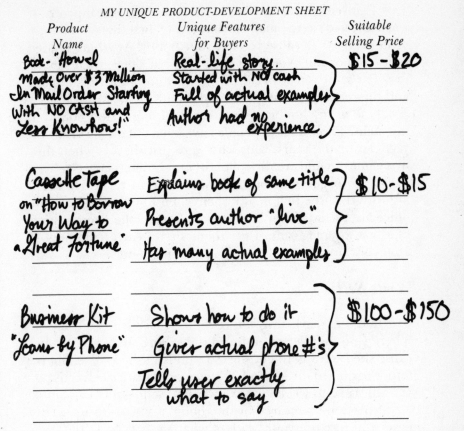

MY UNIQUE PRODUCT-DEVELOPMENT SHEET

Product Name	Unique Features for Buyers	Suitable Selling Price
Book- "How I Made Over $3 Million In Mail Order Starting With NO CASH and Less Knowhow!"	Real-life story. Started with NO cash Full of actual examples Author had no experience	$15-$20
Cassette Tape on "How to Borrow Your Way to a Great Fortune"	Explains book of same title Presents author "live" Has many actual examples	$10-$15
Business Kit "Loans by Phone"	Shows how to do it Gives actual phone #'s Tells user exactly what to say	$100-$150

Figure 2.1 *Typical Portion of a Filled-Out Product-Development Sheet*

- *Specialty stores* interested in handling your item for their customers.
- *Specialized publications* serving the field of your product. If you have an item for brides, *Bride's Magazine* would be a "specialized publication" for your product.

You will often be able to find small, local mailing lists and publications that can make you millions because the unique product you have appeals strongly to the people on the list and the readers. If you find such unique outlets, work them hard! Why do I say this?

Think of yourself. If you have a hobby, you'll probably open any item in the mail on your hobby first, before any other item. Why? Because you *like* your hobby! Anything related to it is important. You want to know what's new, what's exciting. The same is true of the people on your unique mailing list and the readers of the specialized publication.

One of my hobbies is boating on Long Island Sound in my yacht. Thousands of people have been out on my beautiful yachts over the years. Kids who were just shavers when they first came out and are now pilots of big commercial jets tell me "I'll *never* forget those beautiful days on your yacht!" In keeping with this, the first mail I open when I get home from the office are the ads from boating suppliers or the latest edition of a boating magazine (I get them *all!*). Learn from me—I *want* your unique product if it's a boating item!

Write Selling Ads

In direct marketing you're selling directly to your buyer. There's no middleperson to do the selling for you. And because the best way to get started in this business is selling by either (or both) direct mail or space or classified advertising, you will have to write (or have written) selling ads.

Now don't be scared by the thought of writing an ad. It's easy! You just tell your readers what's great about the item you're selling. To sell strongly, a good ad

- *Takes the reader's view*—it tells what's in it for him or her if the item is bought.
- *Emphasizes the positive aspects* of the purchase by the reader, giving *all* the good points.
- *Talks the reader's language,* using the lingo the reader uses when talking about the item.
- *Lists features,* advantages, and savings that the item provides.
- *Uses long copy*—hundreds (or thousands) of words to tell the "whole story" about the item.

To show you what I mean by the features of an ad, I've included two of our recent ads which have pulled well for us—that is, brought in big bundles of orders. These ads are shown in Figures 2.2 and 2.3.

REAL ESTATE MONEY

THE LOW-COST FINANCING ▶ **Success Story**

Zero-cash deals! Owner financing! Long-term loans!

100% Financing! 110% Financing! 120% Financing!

Borrow your way to great success!

Find Mortgage millions now!

Get the cash you need for real-estate deals!

GET ALL KINDS OF REAL-ESTATE LOANS FASTER! Take the hassle and delay out of getting a real-estate loan! How? By using the IWS REAL-ESTATE LOAN GETTERS SERVICE! This NEW service from Ty Hicks gives you:

**Proven ways to get loans
**Forms for fast loan approval
**Names & addresses of lenders
**Step-by-step tips for borrowers
**Keys to getting ANY type of real-estate loan today
**A turn-key business for you in any state, city, or county
**Ways to earn BIG commissions from the easiest loan ever
**Speedy decisions--sometimes in just an hour
**Built-in collateral--no credit check hassles
**Sources of the unusual and hard-to-get real estate loan

100% Financing! 110% Financing! 120% Financing!

YOU CAN USE THIS SERVICE to get loans for your own real-estate deals, or for deals that other people have! Ty Hicks gives YOU complete support in this service--giving you the forms you need, the lenders you can work with, and advice over his hotline!

GET REAL-ESTATE LOANS for any type of deal, from single-family homes to office-complex developments, etc. If it's real estate, this service can help YOU--with 1st, 2nd, 3rd-- even 8th mortgages! Get money for raw land, air rights, shopping centers, garden/senior citizen apartments, marinas!

MEGA-MORTGAGES INTO THE MULTI-MILLIONS are there--just for the asking! Don't let them go to waste! Get in on the real estate boom. Be part of the lending spree that's putting billions into new and used real estate every year! Know who's lending for what use!

TO START USING THIS SERVICE send $100 TODAY to IWS, or call in your credit card order!

SUCCESS STARTS HERE!

Send your check or money order for $100 to IWS, Inc. at the address at the right. Or call Ty Hicks at 800-323-0548 from 9am to 4pm New York time or from 8 to 10 pm at 516-766-5850 with your VISA or MASTERCARD order. If ordering by mail, give card no., expiration date, and your phone number.

MAIL THIS COUPON NOW OR CALL IN YOUR CREDIT CARD ORDER! DON'T WASTE TIME!

Send me the REAL-ESTATE LOAN GETTERS SERVICE. Here's $100. Or charge my credit card at left.

NAME_____ PHONE NO._____

ADDRESS_____

CITY_____ STATE____ ZIP_____

Send to: IWS, Inc. 24 Canterbury Rd
         Rockville Centre NY 11570

To order by credit card, call 1-800-323-0548, day or night.

OVER **OVER** **OVER** **OVER**

Figure 2.2   *Real Estate Loan Getter's Kit*

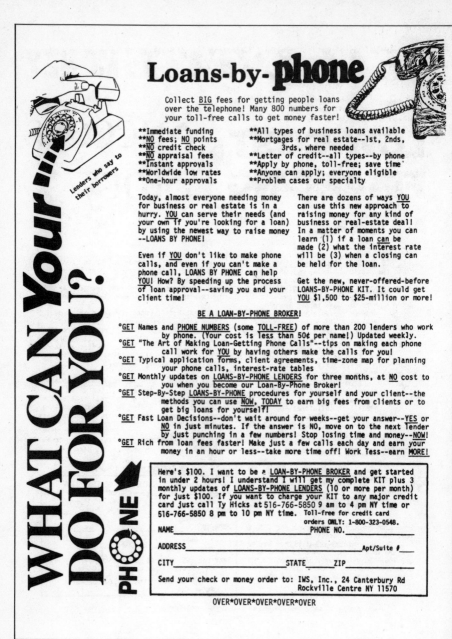

Loans-by-phone

Collect <u>BIG</u> fees for getting people loans over the telephone! Many 800 numbers for your toll-free calls to get money faster!

- **Immediate funding
- **<u>NO</u> fees; <u>NO</u> points
- **<u>NO</u> credit check
- **<u>NO</u> appraisal fees
- **Instant approvals
- **Worldwide low rates
- **One-hour approvals

- **All types of business loans available
- **Mortgages for real estate--1st, 2nds, 3rds, where needed
- **Letter of credit--all types--by phone
- **Apply by phone, toll-free; save time
- **Anyone can apply; everyone eligible
- **Problem cases our specialty

Today, almost everyone needing money for business or real estate is in a hurry. <u>YOU</u> can serve their needs (and your own if you're looking for a loan) by using the newest way to raise money --LOANS BY PHONE!

Even if <u>YOU</u> don't like to make phone calls, and even if you can't make a phone call, LOANS BY PHONE can help <u>YOU</u>! How? By speeding up the process of loan approval--saving you and your client time!

There are dozens of ways <u>YOU</u> can use this new approach to raising money for any kind of business or real-estate deal! In a matter of moments you can learn (1) if a loan <u>can</u> be made (2) what the interest rate will be (3) when a closing can be held for the loan.

Get the new, never-offered-before LOANS-BY-PHONE KIT. It could get <u>YOU</u> $1,500 to $25-million or more!

BE A LOAN-BY-PHONE BROKER!

°<u>GET</u> Names and PHONE NUMBERS (some <u>TOLL-FREE</u>) of more than 200 lenders who work by phone. (Your cost is less than 50¢ per name!) Updated weekly.

°<u>GET</u> "The Art of Making Loan-Getting Phone Calls"--tips on making each phone call work for <u>YOU</u> by having others make the calls for you!

°<u>GET</u> Typical application forms, client agreements, time-zone map for planning your phone calls, interest-rate tables

°<u>GET</u> Monthly updates on <u>LOANS-BY-PHONE LENDERS</u> for three months, at <u>NO</u> cost to you when you become our Loan-By-Phone Broker!

°<u>GET</u> Step-By-Step <u>LOANS-BY-PHONE</u> procedures for yourself and your client--the methods you can use <u>NOW</u>, <u>TODAY</u> to earn big fees from clients or to get big loans for yourself!

°<u>GET</u> Fast Loan Decisions--don't wait around for weeks--get your answer--YES or NO in just minutes. If the answer is NO, move on to the next lender by just punching in a few numbers! Stop losing time and money--NOW!

°<u>GET</u> Rich from loan fees faster! Make just a few calls each day and earn your money in an hour or less--take more time off! Work less--earn <u>MORE</u>!

Here's $100. I want to be a LOAN-BY-PHONE BROKER and get started in under 2 hours! I understand I will get my complete KIT plus 3 monthly updates of <u>LOANS-BY-PHONE LENDERS</u> (10 or more per month) for just $100. If you want to charge your KIT to any major credit card just call Ty Hicks at 516-766-5850 9 am to 4 pm NY time or 516-766-5850 8 pm to 10 pm NY time. Toll-free for credit card orders ONLY: 1-800-323-0548.

NAME_____PHONE NO._____

ADDRESS_____Apt/Suite #____

CITY_____STATE_____ZIP_____

Send your check or money order to: IWS, Inc., 24 Canterbury Rd
                                    Rockville Centre NY 11570

OVER*OVER*OVER*OVER*OVER

WHAT CAN *Your* PHONE DO FOR YOU?

Lenders who say to their borrowers

Figure 2.3   *Loan-by-Phone Broker Kit*

Take a look at these ads, one at a time. Figure 2.2 features what every real estate business person seeks—low-cost financing. And it also gives what every real estate investor seeks—faster money by taking the "hassle and delay out of getting a real estate loan." Then the ad lists ten benefits the kit gives you.

The second ad, Figure 2.3, features ease and speed— "One Call Gets It All." Then it lists thirteen features of the kit that benefit the user. And, it offers ways for the user to earn money with the kit. So there you have it—thirteen benefits plus money! Who could ask for anything more?

Key Secrets of Direct-Marketing Success

There *are* almost no-fail ways to success in direct marketing. I stumbled on them and put them to work. Later I learned that many before me used almost the same secrets to build riches. Some even fly jet planes with the money they earned from these methods. To put money like that into *your* hands, here are the key secrets of direct marketing success:

- *Promote in unusual ways.* Search out unique publications, mailing lists, specialized outlets. Promote strongly through these channels.
- *Be personal in all your marketing.* Talk to your customer like a friend. Work at making your customer your friend, now!
- *Provide speed as part of your product.* Today everyone is in a big hurry. Cater to this speed mania, and you'll make more sales than you ever thought you could.
- *Use credit cards to take orders.* You can increase your business by at least 35 percent by using credit cards. Further, the ability to accept credit card orders gives your business great creditability. People will have greater faith in you!
- *Get an 800 number for orders.* People love to make toll-free phone calls to spend money! So why not have them call *you* to spend money? After all, good friend, that's the whole idea of this effort!

- *Stay open until late at night* to take orders and answer questions. Many people can't get to a phone during business hours. So they like being able to call "after hours" to place orders, get help, or just chat.
- *Don't hide* behind secretaries, answering machines, or other "excuses." Be available—it's good for you and for *your* business.
- *Be easy to talk to.* All of us put on one shoe at a time. So don't think you're superior to your customers! After all, you *do* want them to spend money with you. They'll spend much more if you're easy to reach and easy to talk to.
- *Be ready to deliver quickly.* Use Express Mail or any of the courier services to get your item into the customer's hands faster. Charge the customer the extra delivery cost—they're happy to pay it when you give overnight delivery.
- *Mail, advertise, or promote every day!* Never let a day go by that you don't do something to sell your item(s) or service. You *must* push in this business. If you don't, the competition will knock you out! (I never let a day go by that I don't do something to sell my products. This attitude keeps me in a very nice tax bracket.)
- *Dream up (or find) new products regularly.* New items "turn people on"—make them send money to *you*.

Direct marketing ranges over so many products and services that almost any item you like can be sold this way. For example, a reader who likes the stock market writes:

> A couple of your books were the inspiration that set me off into the newsletter business. I also subscribe to *International Wealth Success.* Started my stock market newsletter six years ago as a one-man operation and have been able to get a $500,000 waterfront home in Florida, a speedboat, a Rolls Royce, and a well-funded corporate pension plan. You're right—it *IS* possible to get rich today—I *did!*

So you see, you *can* pick what you like to sell and sell it by direct marketing. Many people do it regularly and make money while having fun. Thus, one reader who enjoys selling thermometers writes:

I was able to contact a buyer in Canada who wants Celsius [centigrade] thermometers and it looks like a very large order for us—thanks to *IWS* free ads.

(As a subscriber to the *International Wealth Success* newsletter, you're entitled to one *free* classified ad each month—twelve for a one-year subscription, twenty-four for a two-year, and so on.)

Another reader, who has a regular job as secretary and treasurer of a chain of department stores, writes: "I have subscribed to *International Wealth Success*" for several years and have made substantial fees selling businesses in my spare time."

So you see—good friend of mine—you *can* build riches today! And in a business you like. In a business in which you won't be a wage slave. In a business that gives *you* freedom, financial security, and the right to be your own person— starting right now.

Get Rich at Home Today

You *can* make it in direct marketing, starting on your kitchen table. But you won't hit it big unless you develop or find your own unique product, find unusual outlets for it, and keep selling (by mail, through dealers, with space and/or classified ads) while avoiding preprinted catalogs that carry only routine goods that are not unique.

Some people go out and buy thousands of those preprinted catalogs, stick stamps to them, and drop them in the local mailbox. Then they sit back and wait for the millions to pour in. A few have told me they didn't get even *one* sale after spending more than $1000 on catalogs and postage.

The way to start at home is to find that unique first product or service. Make a few sales; then find a second, third, fourth, unique item. Sell it to your earlier customers. Continue along this way as you build your income, week by week.

Remember these important facts about direct marketing, and you'll get rich from your own home:

- Your customer buys a product or service, not your address.
- Customers could care less about your address if they get the item or service they want.
- Your company name, your address (street or post office box) mean little—the product means all.

So spend your time looking for the product that can't be obtained in the store around the corner. Price it high enough to earn a profit while giving value to your customer and you'll get rich—right in your own home. And remember, that home can be an apartment, a van, a motor home, a boat, or a little cottage. It makes *no* difference to your buyer!

So start your business at home. Use a short name for your company—it's easier to print and to remember. Get a local business license from your County Clerk, who's listed in your telephone book. Use *both* your home address and a post office box to receive mail—you'll get *more* mail and *more* checks this way (a Ty Hicks secret I've never revealed before). Apply for a credit card merchant account or use one of the special merchant central accounts that are available to new and small businesses.

Don't Let High Prices Frighten You

For years I've sold excellent business kits, which I developed myself (my unique products), for $99.50. They sold so well—often twenty to twenty-five a week—that I was afraid to raise the price. Then a firm having one similar kit priced at $150 asked me to sell it. I agreed and learned a lot, namely:

- The $150 kit, though nowhere as good as mine, sold fairly well.
- The kit weighed only two pounds, compared to an average of nine pounds for each of my kits, yet people accepted it at one and one-half times the price!
- The service on the kit—in terms of answers and help—was horrible. Yet people kept the kit.

I stopped promoting the kit after three months because the after-sale service was so awful. But selling this one kit taught me several lessons, namely:

- Prices over $100 *were* acceptable to my customers.
- A $100, or higher, priced kit did not have to weigh nine pounds to be worth its price.
- More important, people want speed in results; some may even by frightened by a big pile of reference material.
- Lastly, high prices are *not* a turn-off to people if they feel the product is worth the price.

With postage rates and ad costs rising (except for *International Wealth Success*), you *must* receive a larger amount of money from each sale you make if you're trying to earn a profit. So you'll find higher prices in almost every field of direct marketing.

As other sellers raise their prices, you can too. Remember, *all* direct marketers face almost the same costs. If others raise their prices, you can do the same. So never be afraid of high prices!

[And to finish the story of the above kit with the poor service, I replaced it by developing my own unique (*not* copies) kits that are better, more useful, and are backed by toll-free, 800-number service from me, personally. The result? Zooming sales! All these kits are listed at the back of this book.]

Find a Steady Flow of New Customers

The only other key to direct-marketing success I haven't mentioned is new customer searches. You *must* get a steady flow of new customers into your direct-marketing business. Why?

- Your present customers drop off—they die, get new interests, move elsewhere, and so forth.
- New customers buy more, at a faster rate, than existing customers.
- Without new buyers your business may wither and slowly expire.

Many new direct-marketing wealth builders fail to see the key importance of new customers. So they hoard their money, forgetting that next month's income depends on this month's new buyer. Don't ever let this happen!

How can you get new buyers for your direct-marketing products? There are many ways, including:

- *Run Ads*—either classified, space, or both—in key publications.
- *Rent lists of prospect names* and mail ad material to the names. Be sure to test each list *before* you roll-out— that is, mail to all names on the list you rent.
- *Use low-cost or per-inquiry TV and radio ads* for products having mass appeal. Check out the cable stations—you can often get real bargains there. For per-inquiry (called PI) ads, you pay *only* for each inquiry, not for the time.
- *Get free publicity for your items* in magazines and newspapers by getting product releases, book reviews, and other notices published. You can write such releases yourself using my "Product Publicity Kit" mentioned at the back of this book. Or, you can pay an ad agency to write the release for you.
- *Run free ads* (as a one-year, or longer, subscriber to the *International Wealth Success* newsletter can). Many advertisers report excellent results, such as those below. (People call it *IWS*, for short.)

If you have a unique product that you promote to a unique list, you may be able to report results like these from the *International Wealth Success* newsletter:

> The response to my ad in the January issue of IWS was great. Please run the same ad again.
>
> * * * * *
>
> I have made several worthwhile contacts as a result of reading your newsletter and placing my ads in it.
>
> * * * * *
>
> The enclosed ad can be run every month. We are receiving over 100 replies per month.
>
> * * * * *
>
> Response to our ads in *IWS* has been very good. Thanks.
>
> * * * * *

Most of the people we are now doing business with have come to us through our ads in *IWS*.

I could go on and on, but I think you get the idea. And the above comments come directly from reader letters, sent to us without being requested.

How Much Should a New Customer Cost?

New customers can cost very little or they can cost a lot, depending on how you get them. In general, *new customers* obtained through advertising can be costly, and new customers obtained through free publicity are often obtained for just pennies each.

It's impossible to put a specific dollar value on how much a new customer should cost. But the lower the cost, the better for you! Some rules of thumb used by people who've made a fortune in direct marketing include

- *Half the yearly cost* of a newsletter subscription; thus, a newsletter that costs the subscriber $100 a year is willing to pay $50 for a new subscriber. (Other newsletters are willing to pay as high as one and one-half times — $150 in this case — for a subscriber.)
- *One times the amount of money* the new customer will, on average, spend with us. Thus, if a customer will spend $30 a year, on average, with you, then you'll be willing to spend $30 to get that customer on your list.
- *One-third the sales of a mailing* is acceptable for renting a list, postage, printing, and the like. Another one-third is for product cost. The last one-third is for overhead and profit. This is a rule many direct marketers live by. Thus, with a mailing that sells $4500 per 1000 pieces, you'd be willing to spend $1500 for the list rental, postage, or printing. Another $1500 would go for the making or buying of the product (or service) you're selling. From the last $1500 would come your overhead (rent, light, heat, salaries) and profit.

There are many other rules of thumb. But we really don't have enough room for them here. But one you should keep in mind is this: *If you take a space ad,* you'll make money if the ad returns its cost in sales, if you have other related items to offer your buyer. Thus, if a full-page ad costs $2000 in an opportunity-seekers magazine, it should return at least $2000 in sales. You won't make money on these sales, you'll lose money. But the *additional later sales* you make to these new customers will, if you have related products, bring you a profit!

The key to cost of sales is only you—for your business— can say how much you can afford to pay for a new customer. Just keep in mind this key fact: There are only two ways to raise the profits of a going business—increase sales or cut your costs. The less it costs to get a new customer who increases your sales, the higher your profit will be!

Sell Your Friends a Complete Line of Products

In my business, my customers *are* my friends. Why? Because these are the people who *send me money* to keep me in beautiful yachts and great American cars, *help me pay people* who've worked with me for years and who are fiercely loyal to my business, and *call me to ask questions* about money, their businesses, and "make my day."

Because they all like what they first buy from me, I try to keep them happy by offering them more of the same. So I have (at this writing) a beautiful forty-eight-page catalog showing the many items we have for BWBs. If you've noticed, today is the age of catalog selling, especially for home and electronics items. So I transferred that idea to wealth-building products.

Today, so far as I know, my forty-eight-page catalog is the only one of its kind in the world. (Probably by the time you read this book, there will be a dozen others.) But as of now, it's unique. And we mail it to a unique list of opportunity seekers. These are people who've bought our newsletter or a book from us.

To say that a catalog pulls well is not too accurate. Catalogs pull (make sales) like no other mailings! Why?

- *People keep a catalog* on their desks or shelves for "the day when they'll need that information."
- *People turn to the catalog* when they're ready to buy items that they need for their businesses.
- *People enjoy using the credit card and 800-number* facility that the catalog offers.

There's also another good reason why catalogs sell so well. What's this reason? *Catalogs present a related range* of items, many of which have a good chance of "grabbing the reader." *So when a customer likes your product,* he or she is glad to get information on other related items. *Thus, a catalog becomes a "world"* of a certain line of items. As such, most catalogs are read from cover to cover!

I'll be glad to send you a copy of our forty-eight-page catalog when you buy a book from us or subscribe to our *International Wealth Success* newsletter. You'll enjoy this great catalog, I'm sure!

Keep Your Customers for Years

Earlier I suggested that you make your customers your friends. Why? For a number of very sound reasons:

- *You expand your life* enormously, bringing new people and experiences into your world.
- *Your customers stay with you,* buying more from you, increasing your cash flow and profit.
- *You get ideas from your customers* who say: "Do you have a book on ____?" Or they'll say, "Why don't you publish a book on ____?" The "light goes on inside your head," and you do as your customer suggests.

All my life I've believed in friendly dealings with customers. Why make a customer your enemy when it's easier (and far more profitable) to make your customer a friend? So when people call me on the phone (as thousands do), they often say, "I'm amazed you answered the phone. I thought I'd have to go through ten secretaries before I got to you, if I ever did." My answer is, "Somebody has to answer the phone. And it might as well be me because I enjoy talking to people." So I've made another friend.

And with me, of course, the input from real-life BWBs who are "on the firing line" keeps me in touch with the world. As some of you know, I started my career as a boy of fourteen in the bilges of merchant ships, working as a wiper in the engine room. From there I rose to chief engineer, sailing all over the world. And three of the ships I was on were torpedoed, but I managed to survive.

Today I have readers on merchant ships everywhere. These friends, knowing my background, feel that they know me. And I know them. And they buy and read my books, kits, and newsletters—to their advantage. So keep your customers for years—it pays!

Give Service With a Big Smile

There are thousands of surly, snarling direct-marketing firms in business today. When you call them or write about an order you placed you get a big insult as your answer. Because all of us want to be respected and treated politely, you can build on the poor business practices of others by being friendly and polite at all times, making *every* customer feel welcome when they call or write, and giving a little extra service when you can.

As mentioned earlier, people who call me are amazed that I answer the phone. "You really *can* talk to Ty Hicks," some say in complete disbelief. Then they launch into their questions or stories. Either way, I try to help as much as possible. And I often ask them to call back toll-free on my 800 number to let me know what progress they're making toward their goal.

So learn well, here and now, that service with a smile *can* make you rich! It has built several fortunes for me. And I'm sure it can do the same for you.

Keep Selling Every Day and Night

If you put a sales brochure in the mail, run a commercial on radio or TV, or make a telemarketing call to a prospect, something may happen. My experience is that something *will* happen! Direct-marketing expenses are a *cost* when you must pay the bill. But over a long period these expenses are an *investment*. Why?

- Sales may occur months, even years, after you make the mailing, do the commercial, or make a call.
- Some people may order hundreds of dollars worth of products from just one flyer.
- You're not pushing the limit unless you keep selling every minute of the day.

If you promote day and night, I can almost guarantee that you'll hit the big money if you have a product that helps people. Not only that, other direct-marketing people who see your sales efforts may approach you with ready-made sales. For instance, an attorney who saw just one sentence in a letter I wrote asked me to do mailings for a trade association marketing effort, using a list he compiled of members of the association, attendees to conferences, and the like. This provided him and my firm with a steady and predictable income from direct marketing. Yet if I hadn't sent that letter he might never have approached me to do the work.

Being available to your customers day and night makes them more likely to order from you. Why? They *know* they can get hold of you when they write or call. Other firms are hard to reach, answer only by machine, or don't even have phones! So be available and get rich. It's great fun for everyone.

You *can* mint riches from today's needs. I've done it. And so can *you*, starting right now. Just follow the ideas in this chapter. Add your own twists where you think they'll help. Call or write me if you need help. I'm available day or night— as close as your telephone or mailbox!

CHAPTER 3

MAKE THE WORLD YOUR GOLDEN CHECKBOOK

You can get richer on Other People's Money (OPM) throughout the world—more than you might have ever thought possible! How might *you* build such riches on OPM, starting right now? You can *get into import-export*—one of the most profitable businesses in the world—*starting with little cash* but with great potential. An import-export business is *an ideal "paper" business*, where you need only a mailbox to build your riches.

Get the Centuries in Your Favor

People have been importing and exporting goods for centuries. So if you get into this exciting field, you have more than a 1000 years of tradition behind you. Who could fail in a business that's been making fortunes for this long? You really can't miss—if you start right!

You may not have thought of this before, but it *is* easier to make money on OPM in an established business. Why? *People accept* your business sooner because they've heard of such dealings before, *all the procedures* are in place—you just follow what others have done before—and *financing by letter of credit* is a centuries-old tradition that people know and trust.

Hundreds of my readers have made quick money in import-export—from their very first deal. And most started with just a smattering of know-how and improved as they earned big money. This reader writes:

I made a sale the first time I tried to export. I saw an ad seeking 10,000 billy clubs for an overseas country in *Worldwide Richness Opportunities.* Since there is a firm near me that makes these clubs, I telexed the overseas country that I could supply the items they wanted. They bought 10,000. I'll make about $15,000 on the deal, with an irrevocable letter of credit to my bank.

What this reader really exported were 10,000 billy clubs (night sticks) for the police force of the overseas country. Not a bad profit ($15,000 for his first deal) for helping keep law and order around the world while handling a few pieces of paper!

So if you want to make the world your golden checkbook, get into import-export and licensing, a related field. Let's see how *you* can get started quickly!

Pick a Product You Like

The best way to start making money on OPM in this field is by *exporting*, not importing. Why do I say this? In exporting, *overseas firms* need your products to earn money for themselves. *Such firms pay* with checks that don't bounce (a letter of credit), *while not changing* their minds about the order because it means money to them. *Once you're a trusted supplier,* you'll get many future orders automatically. *Your bank* will give you much *free* help with the paperwork, making things easier for you. *Once you "learn the ropes"* of exporting, it's much easier for you to make a bundle in importing.

Why do I say that you should pick a product (or products) you like? There are very good reasons, namely: *When you like a product,* you have more fun in your business. This *allows you to do a better job* for your customers everywhere, *brings greater satisfaction* and more orders for you, and *helps your business prosper* while building *your* wealth. In picking a product to export, it helps if you know something about the item. Why? Because then you can be more helpful to your customers. Again, this builds your business faster, meaning more money for you.

Find Overseas Firms Seeking Your Product

Once you pick your product to export, get to work finding overseas firms looking for this product. You can do this in several ways:

- *Refer to a copy* of Volumes 1 and 2 of *Worldwide Riches Opportunities* listed at the back of this book. Each volume gives over 2500 overseas firms seeking products to import, which you export to them. The volumes are updated regularly so you have hot leads.
- *Contact the U.S. Department of Commerce* listed in your local phone book under "Government." You can get much helpful information from this agency of the federal government. People at "Commerce" are among the friendliest and most cooperative I've ever met.
- *Contact your state Department of Commerce*, listed in your phone book under "Government." You'll get much help because all states want to increase their exports.
- *Contact international airlines* and steamship firms. A number have lists of export opportunities, available free; all you need do is ask—either in writing or by phone. These leads often are unique, known only to the airline or shipping firm.

Once you find overseas firms seeking the product(s) you want to export, you're ready for the next step. It's an easy one—you just look for local (or distant) suppliers of the product(s) you'll be exporting.

Line Up Your Suppliers

It's best—after you know *what* you'll export and to *whom* you'll export—to line up suppliers of the items. Without suppliers you'll have to make the items yourself. I suggest that you *not* make your export items unless they're very simple—a one-piece tool, a book, or a magazine, for example. Complex items should be bought and resold!

You can find suppliers in a number of different ways. Here are the best for you to use:

- *Refer, in your local library,* to a copy of *Thomas Register of American Manufacturers* for firms that make the item(s) you want to export.
- *Refer, in your local library,* to copies of specialized directories or buyer's guides for the industry you're serving. Thus, the *Chemical Engineering Equipment Buyers' Guide* is an excellent source of names, addresses, and phone numbers of equipment builders in this field.
- *Refer, again in your local library,* to listings of members of trade associations, especially in the fields you want to serve.
- *Read the monthly newsletter* I publish— *International Wealth Success*—for listings of firms with various products available for export. See the back of this book for details on how to subscribe to this great newsletter.

With your suppliers lined up, it's easy to take your next step. But before you do, let me give you some inside tips on this great OPM business.

Insider's Wealth-Building Tips

You *can* make big money on OPM in import-export and licensing. But you must know which products and which areas to look to first. For example, at this time I see great activity in exporting

- Medical and hospital supplies of all types to all areas of the world.
- Instruments and testing equipment, which are popular items in great demand.
- Carpeting, soap, lead pencils, and similar "simple" products (no complicated maintenance), which do well in many export markets.
- Farm produce of all kinds, which is also popular in many areas of the world.

One young reader found an export lead in an issue of *International Wealth Success* (a number are published *every* month) for a new hospital seeking some $800,000 worth of supplies—needles, bandages, tubing, tape, and so on. His commission on this one sale would be 10 percent, or $80,000.

He couldn't find a supplier who would handle all the items (nearly one million) needed by the new hospital. I suggested that he try a small supply source I knew that was hungry for new business. He did, and the hospital supply house agreed to take on the entire order, handle the documents, and do the shipping. My reader was delighted. The commission—his first in exporting— gave him the largest yearly income of his life! Where is the hospital? In Switzerland—one of the most competitive markets anywhere. Yet my young reader got the work.

Some areas of the world are easier (less competitive) to export to than others. Right now I find these areas are

- South America, which seems to be overlooked by exporters; so you'll be welcome there.
- Mexico and Central America, which are also overlooked by exporters.
- Europe—foodstuffs, instruments, and measuring machines sell well.
- Every place that needs specialized products (like the billy clubs mentioned earlier).

Of course, the easiest and the most profitable products to export are armaments—guns, planes, tanks. But I don't recommend that you get into this business! Why? There are strict export controls on such items; such controls make life difficult. Other products, like those mentioned earlier, help people live better lives, they do *not* destroy life. Exporting foodstuffs, carpeting, soap, and the like is easy, quick, simple, without any export controls. So it's much easier to get started in this business!

While you don't need much money to get started in import-export and/or licensing, it's nice to know that you have a good chance of getting the money. This reader writes, "Thank you, Mr. Hicks. Incidentally, I negotiated a $100,000 venture capital loan through the *International Wealth Success* newsletter ad I ran. Thanks, again."

Regular subscribers to the newsletter are allowed to run one free classified ad a month for each month of their subscriptions. Thus, a one-year subscriber gets twelve free ads, a two-year subscriber twenty-four, and so on. See the back of this book for information on subscribing to this great newsletter, which will help you earn more in import-export.

Contact Your Overseas Customer

You now have a *need* (from *Worldwide Riches Opportunities*, Volumes 1 and 2), a *supplier* (from your local library research), and a *desire* within yourself to make money. All you need do is bring the three together with a letter or telex that says, "Gentlemen (or Ladies): We can supply the 1000 test instruments (or any other product you're interested in selling overseas). We'll be glad to quote the price cif (cost, insurance, freight) if you'll tell us where, and how, you want them shipped. We look forward to your reply."

Send the letter or telex to your overseas potential customer and wait for a response. Use air mail when writing— half an ounce doesn't cost that much to send. Be sure to have a *printed* letterhead when you write. It makes the chances of a sale much better. (The envelope should also be printed. But if you're trying to save money, you can get away with a plain airmail envelope at the start.)

Quote Your Price to Your Customer

Once you get a written request for a price quote, contact your suppliers by phone or mail, saying "I have an order for 1000 of your test instruments from an overseas buyer. Please give me a quotation for 1000 of these units cif Santos, Brazil, by air freight, as soon as possible. You can call me at 123–456–7890, day or night. Or, you can reach me by mail at the above address."

Keep after your supplier to furnish you with the cost as soon as possible. Some suppliers take forever to get a quote to you. Remember that your supplier will also make money on the sale. So there's just as good a reason for the supplier to work fast.

As soon as you get the cif price from your supplier,

1. *Contact your overseas buyer*, giving the full price and shipping information.
2. *Tell the buyer* that your supplier is ready to ship immediately when you receive an irrevocable letter of credit covering the cif amount, plus a 10 percent commission on the total price for yourself. Keep your commission amount a secret from both your buyer and supplier.

If your supplier cannot, or will not, furnish information on the insurance and freight components of the cost, have a freight forwarder give you an estimate of these costs. Base them on the weight, volume, and other characteristics of the item(s) you're exporting.

Once you get your irrevocable letter of credit (which will be sent through your bank), contact your supplier. Place the shipment order by writing a short letter, such as "Please ship 1000 Type UV test instruments to ABC Plantation, POB 234, Santos, Brazil. We are holding a letter of credit (irrevocable) for a price of $645 per unit to you. Ship via freight using Speedy Airways service to Brazil. You will be paid as soon as the shipping documents are supplied to me for collecting the letter of credit."

As soon as you have the shipping documents, take or mail them to your bank's international department. You will receive your check in a few days if the papers are in order. Pay your supplier and keep the balance (about 10 percent of the total) for yourself. Then move on to your next export deal!

Sell Hard and You'll Make Money

There are many ways you can make your success in exporting more certain. Use them, starting right now:

1. *Answer trade leads* quickly. Often, the first exporter on the spot gets the order!
2. *Tell the buyer* where you found his/her need so that you qualify yourself.

3. *Show a great interest* in serving the buyer's need in a special and exclusive way.

4. *Give dimensions*, weights, and other physical characteristics in the units used in the buyer's country. Called the SI (System International) System, the most common measurements use meters and kilos.

5. *Give* price and delivery information as soon as you can. Why? Buyers want your items to sell so they can make money!

6. *Ask your bank to get credit information* about a company, if you need it. They'll be glad to do so, free of charge.

7. *Send a copy* of your letter(s) to overseas buyers to the Embassy or Consular post of your country in the buyer's country. People on duty in the embassy or consulate may be able to help you with the sale.

Exporting is much easier than you think. Why? It's really a method of selling by direct mail. And direct selling, as we saw in Chapter 2, is really booming everywhere! So why don't you get in on this boom, now?

Export Without Leaving Home

You can often export without every having to write an overseas letter. Instead you *deal with local branches* of overseas firms, selling directly to them. Shipping and insurance are handled by the local firm, so you don't have to worry about this aspect. You also *sell to local representatives* of overseas countries serving in the nearby embassy or consulate. Again, you just make a local sale, and all the shipping is handled by the foreign rep.

While these ways of exporting *are* simpler than the way we detailed earlier, there are certain drawbacks. First, *there's more competition*—people try the easiest way first. Second, *only the very large firms* have local branches. Often, the best business comes from the smaller firms that need your help. So think twice before you take the easiest way out!

Recognize What You're Really Doing

When you're in business you *must* know what you're doing! Why? Well, if you don't know what you're doing, you may make mistakes. I'm here to stop you from making any silly errors!

The business we're talking about here has two common names. You can use either because they mean the same. You're either an Export Management Agent (EMA) or an Export Management Company (EMC). You're a *middleperson* for the manufacturer (your supplier) and the importer overseas (your customer). You're an *agent* for the manufacturer and for the importer. When you have a number of people working for you the term *export management company* is probably more accurate. Both these terms are recognized by the Department of Commerce. So they're official descriptions of the work you're doing.

As an EMA or EMC you'll be a "wanted" person by many banks. Why? You'll bring business to them. And banks just *love* new business that brings money into their safes. And they'll show their love by lending you money, if you need it. This reader reports

> I was trying to get a loan to buy some real estate but the bank wasn't interested. Then I mentioned to the banker that I had a contract to export one million tons of wheat a year to Africa. He sat right up and said, "You can use that contract as collateral for your real estate loan!" So here I sit with this beautiful real estate that's zooming in value— financed by wheat! You never know what can develop in this business of exporting.

Importing Can Be Profitable, Too

In importing goods or services you are looking for your foreign item to sell better than a competing domestic one. Why might the foreign item sell better? Some reasons are

- Better quality.
- Lower price.

- Attractive image.
- Greater availability.

You *can* make big money in importing. But you *must* be careful because you can wind up with a garage full of unsaleable merchandise. To be successful in importing, follow the rules below. They're based on many years of successful importing, which helped me build a fortune.

1. *Know where* you'll sell your import *before* you agree to bring it in.
2. *Be certain what price* you'll be able to charge for your import and have it sell.
3. *Check out any restrictions* you may meet in importing *before* you bring in one item.

As you might suspect, I highly favor exporting over importing. Why?

1. *There's much less chance* for you to be hurt because the overseas firm needs your product to make money.
2. *Exporting helps* the balance of trade. As a result, you can get a lot of help—free—from the government.
3. *Commercial banks love exporting.* So they'll welcome you as an export customer. As a small-business customer, they might not be too happy with you.

But there are people who want to import. I respect this wish because they might be able to build riches faster than I might. Any skill like that, I fully respect! So let's show these people how to make a million in the importing business, right now.

Know Where You'll Sell Before You Import

Anyone can go out and buy an item to import. But why do this unless you know how and where you can sell the item? Waiting until after you get the item onto the dock before you figure out where to sell it is stupid!

To fulfill this need of knowing where your item will sell, keep these important facts in mind:

- *You must have a specific buyer in mind*. And this buyer should preferably be a store, a company, or a distributor.
- *Never import a product for "everyone."* Why? When you go out to look for "everyone" to make a sale, "they ain't there."
- *Favor a specific-use item over a general-use item*. It's usually better to import a plumber's wrench (specific use and market) than to import a cooling fan for "everyone." Most people might prefer air conditioning over a general fan.

Why do I suggest a specific-use item over a general-use one? The specific-use item customer reads certain magazines in which you can advertise, belongs to certain associations, unions, and the like where you can reach the person, and often has a money (profit) need for buying your import.

Be Certain of the Price You Can Charge

Every product has a certain value to its potential buyers. Your price must be in the value range your buyers place on the item. If your price is too far above this range, you'll lose sales. And if your price is too far below the value range, people will say, "Oh, there must be something wrong with it if it's that cheap. I'll buy the more expensive one!"

How do you know what price to charge for your import? There are a number of ways to find out. Here are a few:

- *Look at the competition*. Price your item somewhat above or below your competitor's price, depending on the relative value of your item — better or less.
- *Price to earn an acceptable profit*. If you're selling to a distributor (someone who will resell the item) charge at least twice your total *landed* cost. For example, an item that costs you a total of $5.00 delivered to your warehouse should be sold to a distributor for *no less* than $10. And if you can get $11 or $12, charge that amount. If you're selling by mail and advertising to the general public, charge at least three times your landed

cost. So, for the above item, you'd charge $15.00 to make a suitable profit.
- *Use your own judgment* when the product has no competition. What would *you* pay for this item, especially in view of its unavailability from anyone else? Then, apply your profit rules.

Check for Import Restrictions

Most items you want to import can be brought in without any problems. But items that may impact the health or well-being of people may have restrictions. Such items might include

- Foodstuffs of various types.
- Animals, pets, other living creatures.
- Arms, ammunition, weapons.
- Plants, trees, flowers.

The Department of Commerce (DOC) can quickly tell you—with just one phone call— if there are any restrictions on your proposed imports. So give DOC a call *before* you start to import. You'll be glad you did.

Use OPM to Build Your Import Wealth

The best way to use OPM to build your import wealth takes a little selling on your part. But you can get started for just a little shoe leather. Here's how:

1. *Decide* what product(s) you want to import to build your wealth.
2. *Find* a local buyer (a company or a distributor) who will give you a written order.
3. *Take* the order to your bank (a commercial bank is best) and ask the bank to prepare a letter of credit for the purchase.
4. *Get* the financing you need to pay for your import, based on the credit rating of your buyer.

Now don't tell me you don't like to sell! Plenty of people don't like to sell. So, as a result, there are fewer people out selling imports than there might be. What does this mean for *you*? It means

- *You have less competition*, so your sales will be easier to make.
- *Buyers will welcome you* because they need saleable products, and you can furnish them at affordable prices.
- *You won't have much resistance* to your sales pitch— people will listen to you!

If you still don't like face-to-face selling, you might want to try my method of selling imports. It eliminates *all* face-to-face selling and substitutes direct mail. And it has made a bundle for me. Here's what you do:

1. *Pick* a product that doesn't take any special selling. (For me this product is technical books published overseas; they can easily be described in a one-page flyer for each book.)
2. *Get* information on your product from your overseas supplier. Many will supply free, printed catalog sheets that you can use almost as is, with just a minor change in the name and address of the supplier.
3. *Figure* where you might mail these to bring in the sales money. (I mail to engineers and scientists in various companies.)
4. *Rent* mailing lists of your potential customers. Send each a flyer about your product. Include an order blank and return envelope.
5. *Watch* the orders (and money) roll it! You're on your way to import wealth on OPM if you use a loan to pay for the product and the mailing.

Build Wealth as a Licensing Agent

Countries around the world want to take shortcuts to commercial success. One way to do this is to get permission (called a *license*) to build items that have been successful elsewhere. Typical items that might be licensed are:

- Electronic products of many different types, both consumer and industrial.
- Medicines, drugs, foods, candies, soft drinks.
- Entertainment products — records, tapes, films.
- Trade names of all kinds.

The overseas firm pays the domestic owner of the patent or trade name a royalty on every item that's sold under the license. *You* get a percentage of this royalty, typically 10 percent for many years.

As a licensing agent you're using OPM as the base of your income. Why is this?

- *Someone paid* to develop the patent or trade name — OPM, not your money.
- *Your sale*, often made by mail, depends on the reputation of the item built by OPM.
- *No money input* is asked of you. You choose how and where you'll market the item.

As a licensing agent you're protected by a carefully worded agreement that spells out what, when, and how you'll be paid for your work. A typical comprehensive licensing agreement is included in my book *How to Make a Fortune as a Licensing Agent*. I'd like to include the agreement here, but we just don't have the room. See the back of this book for information on the above title.

How can *you* make money on OPM as a licensing agent? That's easy. Just take these simple steps:

1. *Decide* what types of products you'll try to license.
2. *Pick* items with which you like to work and about which you have some know-how.
3. *Find* firms that make such products. Do this by referring to the *Thomas Directory* mentioned earlier in this chapter.
4. *Check* overseas firms seeking licensing deals. You'll find these in *Worldwide Riches Opportunities*, Volumes 1 and 2 (see the back of this book); at the Department of Commerce; and, possibly, at your state Department of Commerce.
5. *Call* domestic companies, asking if they're interested in licensing any of their patents or trade names. Or,

you can write them, asking the same question. Keep
careful records of the answers you get.

6. *Contact* by air mail overseas firms needing the type of
   license you're offering. Tell them you have such licenses available.

7. *Get* a price quote as soon as you receive an expression
   of interest from anyone. The price quote will come
   from the domestic company owning the patent or
   trade name.

8. *Send* your overseas customer a copy of your licensing
   agreement, along with the price of the license. Then
   watch the money roll into your bank!

You *can* make *big* money in import-export and licensing.
To get started, just follow the easy tips given in this chapter.
And remember, good friend, I'm always available—day and
night—at the other end of a telephone line if you have any
questions. I'll be glad to hear from you. And I'm willing to
share my know-how and experience. You always have a friend
in Ty Hicks. Try me and see!

CHAPTER 4

GET GLORIOUSLY RICH IN THE BEST TAX HAVEN EVER

YOU'VE SEEN, I'm sure, all sorts of ads telling you how you can live tax-free on some island no one ever heard of before. And I'm sure you wondered then—and still do now—is it worth transferring everything to such an island just to avoid paying taxes?

The answer, good friend, is "No." It isn't worth it! You have the best tax haven ever invented right here in the country where you live. So forget about those exotic islands with their complicated names and laws. Just concentrate on building business in your own area, and you'll get gloriously rich in the best tax haven ever invented! Let's see why I say this and how you can get started.

Get OPM—Tax-Free—To Build Wealth

Money you get from a loan, by public sale of stock, or from a business grant comes to your company *tax-free*. There is *no* tax on a loan, on the sale of stock, or on a grant. So this money flows into your firm's bank completely free of any income tax. Remember the following:

- You do *not* have to report the money you get in the form of a loan as income on your firm's tax return.
- Money from the sale of stock never need be reported on your firm's tax return as income.

- Likewise, money obtained for a business grant never need be reported by your firm.
- And, of course, because money from any of these sources comes to your company, you personally never need report any of the cash flow on your personal tax return.

Of course, you *cannot* use the money you get from these sources as yours to pay personal bills of any kind, unless you receive the money as taxable income. But, the money *can* be used to pay company bills of all kinds—rent, light, heat, salaries, supplies, and so on; buy company long-term assets—real estate, machines, and equipment, for example; and repay back bills incurred by the company during its formation.

All these payments are made free of any income tax. There may, of course, be a sales tax on certain items you buy. But this tax must be paid whether you use after-tax income or tax-free capital from one of the sources mentioned earlier. Sales taxes must even be paid by tax-haven companies.

The key thought for you here may not be too clear. So here it is, stated again: Tax-free sources of money can give you personal access to work-related shelter (office), equipment (typewriters, copiers, computers), transit (autos, aircraft, ships), business dining (restaurants, clubs) that you might not otherwise be allowed to use. Again, you won't be using these items for personal purposes. All usage will be business-related. As such, your usage is *never* taxable. So you see, tax-free OPM can start you on your way to riches. The machines and facilities provided you tax-free can be the tools you use to build quick wealth in today's world.

And no matter what anyone tells you to the contrary, take it from one who does much personal study and consults accounting and legal experts: The new tax law has done little to prevent business people from using the facilities of their business to build wealth. Instead, the new tax law encourages business people to seek aggressive new ways to build riches, using all the methods the law permits. So let's start to build your wealth in your own business—right now! I'll show you how to get rich without killing yourself with work!

Erect Buildings Anywhere With Tax-Free Money

Does your business need an office, a factory, a shopping center? If it does, there's tax-free money "hungry" to be put to work. And you can enjoy the comfort and security of the building, completely tax-free! As someone said in a famous tax-case decision, "Comfort doesn't make a service taxable."

What kinds of tax-free money can *you* get for buildings and other real estate? Here are a few kinds:

- *Mortgages* to cover anywhere from 75 to 120 percent of the cost of the property
- *Construction loans* to erect buildings, stores, factories
- *Rehabilitation loans* (called *rehab* loans) to renovate run-down property of all kinds
- *Conversion loans* to convert a building or site from one type of use to another type
- *Building equity loans* to borrow on the ownership you or someone else may already have in real estate

There are plenty of other kinds of loans you can get for real estate of all types. And every one of these loans is tax-free! The money flows into your bank account without it ever even having to be reported to the tax authorities. Could you ask for anything better?

And, joy of joys, the real estate itself becomes the collateral for the loan you're getting. It even helps you raise money from the public (see Chapter 5), again tax-free.

So if you have a yen for real estate and if you can combine this with your business, you can own that real estate (through your company) tax-free. Any profits from the real estate will be earned by the company. And with the generous depreciation and expense deductions under the new tax law, most of the income will also be tax-free to your company! Great, isn't it?

One reader writes about getting your own business and the real estate related to it:

> We are quite excited and enthused with your ideas and methods concerning success and generation of capital.

We have put a number of your concepts and suggestions to work and have a thriving successful business because of it.

You, I'm convinced, can do much the same. What are you waiting for? There never was a better time to start than right now!

Travel the Way You Like

Business people are entitled to travel for business purposes. Thus, you can make trips to inspect business property; confer, on site, with your managers; interview job candidates; make a sales pitch to potential customers; fire or lay off someone; get direct, on site, information; plus more. And you can travel any way you wish. By that I mean you can travel first class, coach, or economy. You are not questioned as to your class of travel if the travel is for genuine business purposes.

Thus, when I lecture in Europe—bringing money back into our great United States of America—I fly the Concorde over and back. Why? It's fast (just over three hours to cross the same ocean it once took me twenty-three days to cross on a slow freighter), and I arrive refreshed and ready to work. And the work (business) is—after all—the reason I'm on the flight. I go over there to earn taxable income!

Your company can own your means of transportation—an auto, bus, rail car, jet or prop aircraft. Just so long as it's used for business, *all* the costs associated with the vehicle are tax-deductible. And your use of the vehicle is nontaxable to you or your company so long as you use the asset for business purposes.

When we say *all* expenses are deductible we mean fuel and lube oil; insurance; repairs; driver, pilot, or captain salary and benefits; garage, hangar, or dockage fees; plus others. So, as owner of your own business, all these costs are paid for by the business. Nothing comes out of *your* pocket. And as long as you confine your usage to business purposes, you have *no* taxable result of that use!

So ride in luxury. You're entitled, as they say. Your business pays the costs, and you get the comfort. Remember, comfort is not taxable! Traveling the way you like to is an added "perk" from your business, making it more fun.

Build Strong Banking Relationships

"There's nothing as nice as a friend at the bank," remarks one of my readers. "When you need a friend, try to make one at the bank. It can really pay off!" I agree, completely.

When you raise money for your company, you'll have to "park" it somewhere while you get ready to spend it. Most BWBs put the OPM they raise into an interest-bearing bank account. Why lose interest by keeping all the money in a checking account, these BWBs ask themselves. So when you contact a local bank about opening business savings and checking accounts, you'll find *you're a welcome visitor*; there are no steely glances asking what you're looking for. *An assistant vice president* (a dime a dozen in most banks) will guide you to a plush seat and *give complete attention* to your needs without taking time out for phone calls or other visitors. *Your hand will be shaken* as you leave, as an expression of friendship and appreciation.

Why all this friendship? Because you're bringing *money*—that most precious commodity—to the bank. And that's what banks use to earn a profit. The more money they have under their control, the larger the profit they can show. *Banks need you and your business.* Of course, it's the company's money that you're depositing. But banks and banking personnel relate to people first, companies second. So they'll think of *you* as the company, you as a depositor.

You can't use company funds for your personal needs. But the friendship you develop because of the company's deposits *can* and almost certainly will carry over into your personal banking deals. So develop strong banking relationships using OPM. You never know when they'll help. To make these banking ties stronger,

- *Take time* to have the bank personnel remember you; be friendly, courteous, considerate.

- *Be loyal to the bank*—tell people how well they're serving your needs; everyone loves compliments.
- *Spend time* in the bank; get to be known by the staff— it *will* pay off for you!

OPM, again, is the key to your future wealth. And the wise use of OPM can bring riches to *you* faster. One reader writes

> I read and enjoyed your book *How to Borrow Your Way to a Great Fortune.* I used several of your ideas with very good results. I now have a corporation appraised at $2 million and have been operating about fourteen months.

You can build a corporation of this size or more using OPM. Get the banks to help you because you help them. Remember, there's no place better than a bank to have good friends.

Get All Kinds of Personal Business Services

I like to do things in a professional way. That's why I have several expert typists, computer operators, and assorted other people helping me. And I get all these business services completely tax-free. Why? The services these people render me are for profit-making purposes. The money they help me earn is taxable. And I do pay *all* the taxes—Federal, State, City— due and *on time!*

You can have all the business services you need, tax-free. How? *Decide what services* you need to make money now. *Hire* on a full-time or part-time basis the help you need. *Pay these people* from your company funds. *Use an accountant* (paid by your company) to see that *all* the rules on payrolls and independent contractors are followed. In the large firms I often deal with I see all kinds of people on the payroll or on the consulting staff. Thus, I see physicians, dentists, pilots, truck drivers, ship captains, engineers, nurses, accountants, tax attorneys, drafters, plumbers, electricians, and computer jocks, to name some.

What does this mean to *you*? It means that you can get the services of such people for business use completely tax-free.

So long as these people are doing work related to your business, their services are tax-free to you. So you can get the best advice, use the best leased or purchased equipment, work in the most comfortable environment—all tax-free! Why settle for anything less when all this is completely legal? As one reader told me today on the phone,

> I used to do all my own typing on a broken-down manual machine. Now I have a word processor and use it when I'm in the office. And when I'm on the road I send in dictation tapes to my secretary who inputs all my thoughts to the word processor. Life couldn't be better. And the money is rolling in faster because I get my work done sooner, in a more modern form. Thanks for all your generous help and advice. I wish I'd known about you twenty years ago. I'd be much further along than I am right now. But—with your help—I'm sure I'll make the big time much sooner!

Note that this reader's use of his word processor for business purposes is fully tax-deductible. It now only speeds his work; it also gives it the look of a professional. I'd like to hear from you, next!

Put Up an Umbrella for Yourself

Is your credit bad? Do you have some slow-pay records on your credit report? Did you go bankrupt recently? If your answer is "Yes" to any of these questions, you may need a "credit umbrella." What's that? It's an organization (your own business) that substitutes for you (and that poor credit rating) when you're trying to raise money. Thus, it makes it easier for you to get the money you need and reduces (or eliminates) the hassle that you go through when your credit report isn't pristine for years and years.

What can this umbrella (my term) be? It can be any type of organization you choose for your business, such as

- A corporation that takes the services of an attorney to form and costs several hundred dollars.

- A sole proprietorship that you can form yourself and file the papers for a few dollars. I recommend, however, that you have an attorney to prevent the possibility of future problems.
- A partnership, again, that you can form yourself and file the papers with your County Clerk for just a few dollars. But play it safe, get an attorney.

With your organization formed, you use *it*, not yourself when applying for credit of any kind. So your personal credit record does not show up. Plenty of my readers use this approach to credit and get loans, leases, and extended credit of all kinds. Why? Because at the start, your firm's credit record is clean; there are no bad marks on it. Further, with a clean record, there's nothing about which the credit grantor can complain. So most of your applications will be approved, if you can show clear business intentions.

Another interesting aspect of using an umbrella is often overlooked by BWBs seeking to build wealth on OPM. This is you may be asked to sign personally on the firm's credit application (for a loan or a lease, for example), but your credit standing will seldom be investigated. That is, the credit grantor will accept your signature and seldom go beyond it to investigate you personally. Therefore, your own business is not only the best tax shelter ever, but also is a great way to get around a poor credit rating. And this can have more impact on your life than you might realize. Let's see one quick example.

Get All the Credit Cards You Want

If your credit rating is poor and you've tried to get a credit card, you probably struck out. Why? The first step a bank or other credit card issuer takes is to run a credit check on the applicant. Look carefully at any credit card application and you'll see it combines data on yourself with permission for the bank to run any kind of credit check it wishes.

But what happens when a company applies for a credit card? Especially if that company has a perfect credit record?

The card is usually approved, and the company winds up with a way to buy items on credit! Because you're the principal in the company, *you* can do the buying in any of the thousands of places where cards are accepted.

And if you're at a loss as to which credit card issuer to approach, get a copy of *Money Raiser's Directory of Credit Card Programs* listed at the back of this book. It gives you some 500 banks around the world that issue credit cards plus their employment requirements, income levels needed, interest rate charged on card purchases, and other key data on their credit cards. With this information in hand you can pick and choose those cards you want. There's no need to go begging. With your cards you can get a strong line of credit on *each* card, borrow money for business use, and get the supplies you need— sooner.

Credit is truly the way to wealth on OPM. And credit cards are today's way to quick results. You can become a "plastic millionaire" using the credit cards obtained through the world's best tax shelter—your own business!

Work With UDAGs and LVFs

Today is the age of the acronym—an abbreviation that's somewhat pronounceable. That's what UDAGs and LVFs are! A UDAG is an Urban Development Action Grant—money given to your company to do something worthwhile in the area like creating new jobs for workers, erecting a new building in the area, and developing housing, industrial, or commercial complexes. You can't get a UDAG as an individual. But as a company, you're as eligible to apply as anyone else! So, again, having your own business can mean big bucks to you.

Where will your firm apply for a UDAG? The best place is your local Economic Development Agency. Look it up in the telephone book. Call around. Its name may be slightly different. But the purpose is the same—to develop the local area to increase the number of jobs, businesses, and so on.

LVFs are Landmark Venture Funds—money that's

available in many large cities to restore buildings, parks, roads, and the like that have historic interest and value. You can't get these funds as an individual. But you *can* get them as a company if you do the type of work required. Again, the advantage of having your own business!

Where do you apply for Landmark Venture Funds? Try your local development agency. Again, you'll find it in the telephone book for the nearest large city. Look up under "City and State Government." And start calling! In three or four calls you'll have narrowed it down to the right agency. You can, of course, write, but this takes longer. And most BWBs I meet want their money fast, so they phone.

Build Multi-Income Sources

The nicest feeling in life is when you have money "coming from all directions." Why?

- Money coming from several sources makes you richer, faster.
- You worry less when you know that you have multiple income sources.
- You seem richer (and really are) when there are a number of income checks arriving every week or month.
- You have greater financial freedom in spending, buying, saving, and investing with income checks arriving from many sources.

To show you what I means by this, I want to quote from a reader letter. It summarizes the benefits you gain from multi-income sources in your own business, financed by OPM:

> I used information from your books to open an indoor miniature golf course. Through continued use of your techniques I expanded the original establishment to include a full arcade. And I opened my second amusement center last year. It, too, is making money for me.
>
> Just when I thought I mastered your techniques, you did it to me again. In an issue of *International Wealth Success* earlier this year, you suggested that every business should develop a second source of income. I thought

about that awhile and realized there was no handbook telling people all they need to know to open an indoor mini golf and arcade business. Though I never wrote a book before, I decided to follow your suggestion and give it a try.

The result is the book *Quarterly Dividends—A Handbook of Arcade Operation.* I want you to know that you are responsible for the idea that led to its creation. I'm planning to sell it for $15 a copy.

This reader did three things. He opened more than one business in the same place (indoor golf and arcade machines). Then, he went another step further and opened the second business, giving him *four* sources (two indoor golf courses and two arcades) of income. Not satisfied with that, he wrote the handbook, giving him a fifth source of income!

With these multi-income sources, this reader never need worry. Why? Because when one business is down, the others can be up. Thus, he has a steady source of money coming in from all directions.

You can do the same. Just pick a business that can develop multisources of income. People who sell our newsletters and books as executive reps get instant multisources of income because the newsletters and books cover so many different topics that they can appeal to a wide audience. (See the back of this book for information on Publisher's Executive Representative Plan.)

Be an Agent for the Unusual

With your own business you can engage in any legal activity that will make money for you. Thus, one good friend of mine builds ship models. These are so popular at prices from $1400 to $25,000 each that he can't keep up with the demand. The gallery owners through whom he sells his models are constantly after him to build more models so they can sell them. Their commission, by the way, is 50 percent of the selling price. So they need "product" to keep eating regularly.

On a recent trip to Europe this model maker had a sudden idea, suggested by my urging him to develop multi-income sources. The idea was to bring ship models from Europe to the United States completely at his (my model-maker friend's) risk. The demand for ship models in Europe is almost nil. Yet European ship models are superbly built. Collectors in the United States would go bonkers over the models. Putting the models in galleries would give my friend multi-income sources dealing with the unusual. I urged my friend to get started because his idea had all the elements of success, namely:

- It's based on OPM—the European model maker's time and energy (= money!).
- It's based on the unusual—ship models that are accurately built are hard to find in the United States.
- It will give the model maker here an extra source of income.

He launched his model importing business, and it's going great! Galleries all over are bugging him to find more fine models to bring in, which they can sell quickly to earn a big profit. Everyone is happy—the overseas model maker (who now has a ready market), the gallery owners (who now have a source of product that's good and reliable), and my model-maker friend who's doing the unusual to earn an extra buck!

Now I know ship models may not be your "bag," but there are probably other unusual items you can handle as an agent in your own tax-haven business. Why not sit down, right now, with pencil and paper and list unusual items for which you might be an agent. It could make you a millionaire.

And, P.S., did I buy any of the ship models? Sure did! My office is decorated with them. Because as you know, as a boy I sailed on twelve different merchant ships over an eight-year period. I saw almost all of this great world of ours. So my mind is often "out there" at sea, thinking about those ships and my friends on three of them who never made port. There's nothing as effective as an accurate model to give a sense of "being there." That's why they sell so well.

For Instant Shelter, Buy Your Tax Haven

Suppose you don't want to take the time to start your own business. What then? You can always buy a *going* business and have income the same day you buy the business; get the fixtures, space, and equipment instantly; have trained people available, where there's a payroll; and, get customers immediately.

Buying a business can be a fast way to your tax haven. But you *must* know *why* you want a specific business, *what* its profits will be for you (they're almost always less than the buyer thinks they'll be), *which* of several offers is the best buy, and *when* you can get the business for the least cash. Here are some tips on buying your business:

- *Know* what kind of business you'll be happy running. (It's really more important to be happy in the business than having the potential of making millions. Being happy in the business will bring in the millions later.)
- *Get to know* the numbers of your future business. *Every* business has a typical or average profit per dollar of sales. *Know* what this is for your business.
- *Never buy the first business* you look at until after you've checked out other, similar businesses. Why? Emotion can rule your thinking when you buy without first looking at other businesses.
- *Never pay the asking price*. Every seller—no matter what is said— expects the asking price to be lowered by the buyer. So what does the seller do? He or she *raises* the asking price to a level that allows it to be lowered by the buyer to the level where the seller gets what he or she really wants!
- *Never buy a business without an attorney* to guide you. You're playing with fire if you skip having the advice of a competent attorney. In every business I've bought (and I'm still buying them), an attorney has been at my side, step by step. And the fee I paid was well worth the sound and helpful advice the attorney gave me.

For best results when buying a business, get a notebook. Enter in this notebook full data on every business you look at. Data should include:

- Asking price; amount of down payment.
- Annual sales; annual profits.
- Annual expenses; rent; salaries, and the like.
- Length of time in business.
- Why the seller wants out.
- Money owed on various bills.

Getting information on six or eight businesses will make you an "expert" on the numbers for that *type* of business. You'll quickly see a rough relationship between the price and profits of each business. Also, you'll be able to see which business offers more to you per dollar of price.

Try, as much as you can, to get the business for no down payment. That's using infinite OPM. And it *can* be done. To work work what I call a zero-cash deal, take these steps:

- *Work out* the lowest down payment possible.
- *Be willing* to pay a little more in the total price for a reduced down payment.
- *Borrow*—on a signature loan, from your credit card line of credit, or from relatives and friends—the down payment on the business.
- *Get the seller* to finance the balance over a three- to seven-year period—the longer the better. Include a no-penalty, early-payoff clause so that you can pay for the business sooner if you have the cash.
- *Run the business* to pay off its debts as soon as possible.
- *If you take on any business debts* from the seller, use these to reduce the cash down payment. Then try to get the debts reduced for a quick payoff. This can lower the total cost of the business to you.

One smart tip you should keep in mind when buying any business from any seller is when you're looking in the classified ads in local newspapers for a business to buy, look in both the "Available" and "Wanted" columns. Why? In the "Wanted" columns, a prospective buyer will often tell what he or she wants a business to have. This information can be a clue as to what the business you want to buy should have. Without such a clue, you might overlook important items your business should have.

Once you buy your first business, you can—after you get to know it—expand to a second, third, and so on. Each new business gives you greater tax freedom and more independence. Also, your income will rise as each business delivers more profit to you.

And, if you organize your business carefully, you can easily run it as an *absentee manager*. This means you need not be in your place of business every day. Instead, others can run the business for you while you're out looking for new ways to build your riches on OPM.

Grab Your Success Now

Truly, friend, owning your own business financed on OPM can be the greatest opportunity of your lifetime. So grab your success now. There never was a better time than today, this very moment, right here!

And if you run into any problems, you always have your good friend—Ty Hicks—as close to you as your telephone, day and night! While I can't solve every problem on the spot, I *do* promise you this: Tell me what your business problem is, and I'll work to solve it. I haven't found a business problem yet that I couldn't solve in twenty-four hours or less. And I'll call you back, free, with the answer! So start getting gloriously rich in the best tax-haven ever. You deserve to be wealthy and to become a money master using OPM!

CHAPTER 5

HOW TO BE FLOODED WITH CASH TO BUILD WEALTH

THE WHOLE KEY to building wealth on OPM—Other People's Money—is to be able to control cash. Why? When *you* control cash, *you* direct its use. This means that you can pick where you'll invest the money. With such control comes power and wealth.

So your main job in building wealth with OPM is locating and controlling that OPM. Loans, as we saw earlier, are one important source of OPM. And you'll use loans again and again during your business life.

But loans *must* be repaid! So you have the monthly "nut" of the loan payment. Suppose you could get as much or more money as in a loan without the monthly loan payment? Without ever having to repay the money? A dream? No! You *can* be flooded with cash that never need be repaid. Let's see how.

Understanding No-Repay Funding for Your Wealth

The whole idea behind any business is to make money grow. Thus, if you put $1000 into a business, you hope to see it grow through sales to $2000, $4000, and up. When money grows through profits, you benefit because you have more money to spend. And the firms whose products you buy when you spend money also benefit. Before long, we have a strong, growing economy!

But suppose you didn't have that $1000 (or $1 million, or $50 million) to invest in your business? You might go to an investor (someone wanting to see his or her money grow) and say:

> "I have this great idea for a business. But I need $1000 to get started. If you'll invest that money in this business, I believe I can make it grow to $4000, or more. Are you interested?"

When you ask such investors for money it's called "going public." That is, you're asking the public to invest in your business. (You can also go public in private. That's covered later in this chapter.) Investors who put money into your company do so by buying a portion of the company. You sell only enough to get the money you need *without* giving up control of your firm!

Why Going Public Is Good for Your Business

Most BWBs, when first learning about raising money from the public, worry about losing control of their business. Forget it! You *can* easily retain control while having "buckets" of money to use for your business. And, good friend of mine, companies go public and raise big money:

- Even *before* they've made one dollar in sales.
- When their *only* history is one of bills paid to start the company.
- *Before* they've assembled their entire management team to run the company.
- With little more than a good business plan that tells what they plan to do.

Going public gives your business many advantages that being private does not have. These are as follows:

- You get instant operating funds to operate your business to bring in the profits.
- As a public company your business has greater credit-ability—investors believe in it.

- Once you raise money from the public, you can always go back for more, getting "second-round" financing.
- You can get more help from banks and other lenders because you'll have money to keep on deposit with them.

So going public *is* good for your company! And let me say that it's also *great* for your firm's pocketbook. Why? You're running the company on OPM—Other People's Money—that *never* need be repaid! Could you ask for any better deal?

What You Need to Go Public

While going public *is* easy, it *does* take some work on your part. But I'm here to help with this work—with good guides and personal advice. So you're not alone!

To go public you need a business plan. When your business plan is converted into a document that's distributed to the public, it's called a *prospectus.* Don't let the word frighten you—it's still your business plan!

Now don't turn away from going public just because you need a business plan. A business plan is needed by every person wanting to build wealth. Why? A business plan tells:

- What business you plan to enter.
- Who will buy your product or service.
- Where and whom your competitors are.
- Why you think you can make a bundle in the business.
- Which products or services will bring what income.

After resisting the need to "do" a business plan, one happy reader told me recently

> It wasn't until I sat down and sketched out my business plan that I really saw my future. I know I resisted you for pushing me into doing the plan but I now see you were right. The plan made all the difference when I started to raise money. And it helped me have all the answers on hand when the questions started to come in!

You can easily do your business plan, using the brief outline above. Just add to it information on the company managers—you and anyone with whom you'll be working. Give data on your education and business experience. Show why *you* can make a success of the business.

Make financial projections—your sales for the first year, second year, and third year. How do you do this? It's simple:

- Figure out how many products or services you'll sell each month of the year.
- Convert these sales into dollars of income for your company.
- Total the sales for each month to give you the year's sales.

What you've just prepared is called your *sales budget*. Because it takes money to make money, you'll also need an *expense budget*. Prepare your expense budget the same way, namely

- Figure out your monthly costs for rent, light, heat, salaries, materials, travel, and the like.
- Add up your monthly expenses to give you the year's expense total.

If you're to show a profit in your business, your yearly expenses must be less than your yearly sales. The difference— roughly—is your yearly profit. As your company becomes more profitable (earns more after expenses), investors place a higher value on its shares. This value is what investors pay for when they buy stock in the public market.

Know How Much Money You Need

The next step in going public is to determine how much money you'll need for your company. To determine how much money you need, take these easy steps to bundles of company money:

1. *List* what items (machines, buildings, tools, for example) you'll need for your business.

2. *Get,* or estimate, the price of each item you'll need; enter this price alongside the item name.
3. *Decide* what other funds you might need to repay company debts, to pay salaries while your firm gets started, to pay research costs, to pay for expenses (travel, postage, telephone, for example). List the exact amount you'll need for each expense.
4. *Total* all your estimated costs to get your company running and making money.
5. *Apply* a safety factor (as we engineers say) of one and one-quarter times your estimated amount of money needed. This is a 25 percent safety factor, one that I've found works well for almost every business.

To see how this might work for you, let's say that you determine you need $1 million of public money to get your company rolling. But, as we all know, estimates can be wrong. So you apply the Hicks factor of 1.25 and decide that you need $1.25 \times \$1,000,000 = \$1,250,000$. This is the amount of money you'll raise from the public for your company!

Pick the Best Way to Go Public

You can go public in just your own state (called *intrastate*) or nationally, in all states. In helping young and new firms go public, I find that the firm that goes public nationally:

- Raises more money for its work and its management team and staff.
- Has an easier job of finding a stock broker (also called an *underwriter*).
- Gets its money faster.

Why do I say this? Because the work that you do for an intrastate sale of stock is basically the same as the work you do for a national sale. So why not get the advantages of the national sale?

To go public nationally, you should use the Securities & Exchange Commission (SEC) *Regulation A* method for small firms. It allows you to raise many millions of public money easily and quickly. Further, it's designed for new small firms that might not have any sales history. You can get full information on going public with Regulation A from my "Financial Broker Kit." (See the back of this book for full details.)

Steps in Getting Your Public Money

You must follow a plan to get public money if you want to have a pleasant and successful experience. Here's the plan I use with BWBs. It works regularly for them. So I have high hopes that it will work for *you,* starting right now! Here's *your* plan:

1. Write, or have someone write, the prospectus (business plan) for you. This is easy because the Regulation A information you get in the "Financial Broker Kit" gives a full outline of the information wanted by SEC in any prospectus.
2. Have your prospectus checked by an attorney you plan to have guide you in selling corporation shares to the public. Follow the advice the attorney gives you concerning your prospectus.
3. Find a stock broker who will take your company public. Do this by sending your prospectus to brokers who specialize in taking new small firms public. These brokers do "Initial Public Offerings," called IPOs for short. If you can't find a brokerage house locally, order a copy of my *Wall Street Syndicators,* listed at the back of this book. It gives you hundreds of brokers who will consider taking you public. The listing also gives summaries of many new firms, showing what they list in their prospectus filing. It will help you understand better the world of public money for growing companies.
4. Work out a deal with the broker as to the cost to your corporation for the public offering. This cost includes printing, advertising (tombstone-type ads), legal opinions, "back-office" work, and the like. The total cost usually runs 15 percent or less of the money raised. Thus, if your public offering raises $1 million before expenses, the cost to your corporation will be about

$150,000. You do *not* pay this money. Instead, it comes out of the proceeds of the offering. So if you can work out a deal for 12 percent, more money stays in your corporate bank account. And don't be afraid to negotiate — stock brokers need new public offerings to keep themselves in yachts and minks!

5. Follow *all* legal procedures recommended to you. Going public is easy but you *must* step very carefully so you don't stub your toe on one of the complex rules that govern the process. So listen to the attorney. As a trained professional, the attorney has only your safety in view! Don't think that you know it all — no one does.

6. Get your money and start building your company. Remember that the reason you raised the money is to make it grow for yourself and others. So start building fast. The earlier your start, the sooner you'll show good results. And these results will help you raise more money sooner.

Working With Your Broker for Best Results

Many BWBs who call me or visit me in my office in Rockefeller Center in New York City find it hard to believe that

- You *can* go public and get money even though you've never made a dollar in sales.
- You *can* go public with a company that has nothing to its name but debts (money it owes) incurred while being formed and started.
- You *can* go public to raise money to pay off these debts and become solvent.

Sometimes its seems to me that the most attractive public offerings are those firms that owe the largest amount of money! Crazy, but true.

You can overcome all sorts of company problems — debts, product failures, bankruptcy — by working with your broker. Why?

- A good broker has strong connections on the "street" with people who might be willing to back you.
- Brokers can help you get around earlier problems. The broker's view is that the person with business problems *did* try. So he or she is a doer. And there aren't that many doers in this world. So why not back this one (*you*) despite these earlier problems?

To work with your broker, you *must* "move with the flow." That is, you must listen to the broker and, in general, do as he or she recommends. Don't fight your broker. You'll just lose out. And you may miss the biggest opportunity of your lifetime. So *listen* to the broker. *Do* as you're told. If you feel like telling someone off, wait until next time when you have more to offer. For now, take the orders!

Taking Your Company Public Yourself

Suppose that you're an independent cuss and you want to do everything yourself. Can you still go public? You certainly can. And many firms *do* go public themselves. They save much of the 15 percent costs mentioned above. But, as the man said, "There ain't no free lunches." This is true of going public yourself. Why? While you save most of the 15 percent in fees and expenses, you also must do a lot more work!

How can you go public yourself? It's easy. You just do all the work the broker does, including selling the shares of stock in your corporation. Remember, good friend, your business *must* be organized as a corporation to sell shares of stock to the public. (In a bit, I'll tell you how you can go public as a partnership.) So, to go public yourself, take these easy steps:

1. *Write* and have typed your prospectus. It need not be typeset—typewriter composition is acceptable. And if you don't want to write the prospectus yourself, hire someone to do the writing.
2. *Register* your stock offering by filing copies of your prospectus with the appropriate agency (SEC for a national offering, your state for an intrastate offering).

Follow, *exactly,* the guidance of a knowledgeable attorney. You *must* have an attorney to go public. His or her fee can come out of the proceeds of the offering.

3. *Sell* shares of stock in your corporation to friends, business associates, and others as soon as your prospectus is approved. You need *not* be a registered stock broker to sell shares in your own firm, one in which you're an elected officer.

4. *Deposit* the money you get in an escrow account in the name of your corporation. Go on to raise the money you need. Watch how friendly your banker becomes. The former cold-fish look turns into a beaming smile as he or she puts his arm around your shoulder and gently leads you to a plushly furnished office to tell you how much the bank values your business!

A number of my readers have taken their companies public. One did it as a financial broker—a business that's almost a one-person operation. Yet this BWB took his firm public, got it listed on the Over-the-Counter (OTC) market, and went on to raise more money! All with a typed prospectus that he banged out himself on a broken-down typewriter. Today his office sports the newest electronic machines, and any future prospectus will be typeset by a compositor.

In summary, to go public yourself, get an attorney! Armed with this guidance, you should be able to raise the money you need—from $300,000 to $5 million for your first effort, with plenty more after that.

Are we really talking *big* money for going public? We really are! For example, in a recent five-year period, new stock issues raised $55 billion—that's an average of about $1 billion a month! So you see, there's really a lot of money being raised by new businesses to fund their expenses and growth. Why not make some of those billions yours?

Private Offerings Can Give You "Speed Money"

A *private offering* is handled by a stock broker. Your shares are sold quickly to investors the stock broker knows.

Millions are raised in private offerings *overnight!* That's right—millions in twenty-four hours or less.

To do a private offering, you follow the same steps as given above for a public offering. But:

- You tell your broker that you want a private offering instead of a public one.
- To raise money quickly so you can get your business started.
- You save money because the expenses to the brokerage house are much lower in a private offering than in a public one.

All the broker need do is phone a few investors and sell your shares. It's as easy as that! So your costs (and the broker's) are much, much lower. You wind up with more money, quicker.

What amounts of money will a private offering (also called a private placement) raise? Millions. Here, in front of me, I have the announcement of a private placement that delivered $23.5 million to the company. And that's *not* the biggest I've seen.

So you *can* get *big* money through a private placement. Why not start *now* getting your offer ready for a suitable brokerage house? It could really make a big difference in the life of *your* company!

Tap the Public Till With a Partnership

If you don't want to operate as a corporation but still want to raise money from the public, consider a partnership. A partnership—usually sold as a *limited partnership*–can raise money either by public or private offering. And the bucks you can get can really be big! Thus, during the recent five-year period mentioned above, partnerships of all kinds raised $80 billion. That's an average of $1.33 billion a month! Real big bucks in anyone's language.

To get money for a limited partnership (usually the best business form for raising money from the public till), take these steps:

1. *Find* a qualified attorney who's willing to draw up the partnership papers. This is really an easy task for experienced attorneys because they usually just refer to a past deal and "make it the same but different."

2. *Pay the attorney* out of the proceeds of the offering. This means you won't have to lay out any money now.

3. *Write* (or have written) your business plan for the partnership. Do *not* make your partnership a tax-avoidance scam! Instead, structure your partnership to be a legitimate profit-making deal. That's what people—and the IRS—want these days. (And it's what I've *always* recommended in all my writings. Why go into business to *lose* money? Any idiot can do that! Go into business to *earn* money—that's the major purpose of any business.)

4. *Register* your business plan in the form of a prospectus with the SEC or your local securities agency. Your attorney will usually handle this for you. If you'd like to see a typical example of a real estate limited-partnership business plan/prospectus, order my "Starting Millionaire Success Kit," K-2, at the back of this book. It will help you a lot. And, by the way, the real estate limited-partnership is probably the most popular type. With it you can raise millions of dollars to buy, develop, or improve real estate.

5. *Sell* (or have someone sell) participations in your partnership. Typically each participation is priced at $5000 to $50,000. So if you sell 100 participations at $50,000 each, your partnership will have $5,000,000! Not bad for getting a profitable business going.

6. *Appoint yourself* general partner. This means that you will run the business and issue periodic reports to your limited partners. It also means that you're the boss and that you want those other people to let you run your show! (A limited partner can't be held responsible for any more than the amount of his or her participation, if the company is sued for any reason.)

7. *Go to market,* even if you don't know what the partnership will invest in (called a *blind* pool). You can always invest the money you raise (called *parking* it) in safe Certificates of Deposit or some other insured type of instrument. Then the money will be earning interest for the partnership while you look around for a secure type of investment that will grow and pay the partners a worthwhile profit.

8. *Keep in touch* with your limited partners by making regular mailings to them, telling them what's going on. You can use a regular typewriter for this work. But if you have a personal computer you can program it to print labels and letters or memos for keeping in touch. You can also use the computer to analyze investment offers to see what kind of return you'll earn for your partners. There are many software programs available to do this analysis quickly and accurately.

9. *Get ready* for your second partnership offering as soon as the first begins to make money for its partners. Why? If your partners make money, they'll tell their friends (at the country club, the yacht club, and athletic clubs, where such investors go to relax). And their friends will be hot to invest with you. So get them while they're in the mood—offer them a second (and a third, fourth, and so on) partnership to help build their wealth.

10. *Branch out* to other profitable fields so that you offer your investors more variety. Typical profitable fields for limited partnership offerings to the public include real estate of all types; equipment leasing— aircraft, trains, ships, and autos, for example; oil and gas exploration and production; computers, copiers, typewriters, and telephone systems; medical and dental equipment for all types of professionals; and energy resources—coal mines, local power plants, and so on.

11. *Build your banking connections* by placing the partnership funds in sound, aggressive, and ambitious banks. Doing so will ensure that the banker remembers your name the next time you stop by to visit!

Use a Finder to Speed Results

Suppose all the steps I outlined above turn you off? Yet, you still want to raise money from the public instead of taking out a loan. What can you do? You can hire a finder to do most of the work for you. Thus, a finder will—for a fee paid *after* the work is successfully performed—do the following:

1. *Prepare* a prospectus or find someone who will do this work.
2. *Search* for a brokerage house that will be interested in taking your firm public.
3. *Negotiate* with the brokerage house for the lowest cost deal for you.
4. *Introduce you* to the best brokerage house for your stock sale.
5. *Step out of the picture* when the deal starts to move toward completion.
6. *Collect the agreed-on fee* from you, *after* you have the funds from the sale of your stock.

The finder does the leg work, acting on your instructions. If you have a marketable deal, the finder will work without any deposit or payment from you. Why? Because the finder knows the money will come in the day after the public offering is finished. So the finder doesn't have to worry about being paid.

Finders are used by many firms going public for the first time. To verify this, I suggest that you read a few new-firm offering circulars as the prospectus is sometimes called. You'll often see the following paragraph (or one similar to it) in the offering circular:

> A finder's fee of $500,000 will be paid to A. B. Doe on successful completion of this offering for work done in connection with the offering. This fee is covered by a Letter of Agreement between A. B. Doe and the corporation, executed prior to the date of this offering. Payment of the fee will be made from the proceeds of the offering within 24 (twenty-four) hours after completion of the offering. The fee will be paid to A. B. Doe in the form of a certified check drawn on the corporate account.

How and Where to Find Your Finder

There are a number of productive publications in which you can advertise for a finder if you can't find one among your business associates. To find a qualified finder,

- *Ask business associates* who might have worked with a finder to recommend one to you.
- *Advertise in suitable media,* such as the newsletter *International Wealth Success* (see the back of this book for details), the *Wall Street Journal,* or your local large-city newspaper. Write a short classified ad that reads thus:

  Finder needed to take new company public. Generous fee on successful offering. Call 123-4567 day or night.

  Or your ad might say:

  Earn big finder's fee for taking new company public. For full details, call 123-4567 day or night.

- *Contact* local small-issue stock brokers. Ask if they can recommend a qualified finder. Then contact the finder yourself and make an offer after describing the work that must be done.

Note that you don't have to pay a finder all cash. You can, if you wish, pay part of the fee in the form of stock in your corporation. This reduces the cash drain from the money you raise.

Once you have a suitable finder, you *must* get a written agreement (called *Letter of Agreement*) signed by the finder. Why is this?

- Without a written agreement, all sorts of misunderstandings can arise, leading to lawsuits.
- The written agreement tells everyone—including you—what will be done, by whom, and for how much.

Have your attorney prepare the finder agreement. If the attorney hasn't seen such an agreement, here's an example of the typical wording used:

FINDER AGREEMENT*

The XYZ Corporation (your firm) hereby agrees to pay John Finder (or Mary Finder) a finder's fee of $500,000 for the following work on its successful completion: (1) finding and signing an agreement with a brokerage house to take XYZ Corporation public with the sale of $10 million in shares; (2) introducing the undersigned (you) to the principals of the brokerage house selected; (3) assisting in any other way that the parties agree to in mutual conference. The fee described above will be paid to John Finder (or Mary Finder) within 24 (twenty-four) hours after the completion of the public offering of the stock of XYZ Corporation. If the stock is offered on a best-efforts basis, the fee will be paid on completion of the best-efforts sale.

Agreed:

Your Signature

_____   _____
XYZ Corporation   Date

John (or Mary) Finder's Signature

_____   _____
Finder   Date

Remember, have *your* Finder Agreement written by your attorney. Only then can you be sure it protects you and your firm.

How to Turn Pennies Into Greenbacks

A public stock offering allows *you* to turn pennies into greenbacks almost overnight! Most public offerings take less than ninety days. This means that with just a few pieces of paper to describe your company and your business ideas, you *can* get the money you need to build wealth.

Thousands of BWBs have taken their companies public,

*This can also be used for private offerings and partnerships; change wording to suit.

and thousands more will. The hunger of the public for new companies that will become the next Xerox, Apple Computer, or Seagate Technologies is beyond comprehension. And your firm *can* be the next one to sweep the market off its feet.

Just remember to go about your public offering in the *right* way. Be sure you and your firm have

- A competent attorney to advise you *every* step of the way.
- A clear view of your market, your competition, and your skills.
- A stated mission for your company that will guide it through the shoals you're sure to encounter.
- A firm determination to win, no matter what the odds!

Yes, a public company *can* make you richer, faster. Why not start *today* to take the necessary steps to get *your* public company? It could put you on easy street for life, using OPM.

You *can* be flooded with cash that you control—all from OPM obtained with a public or private stock offering. You now know how. What are you waiting for? Go from flat broke to great riches sooner on OPM!

CHAPTER 6

MAKE A FORTUNE WALKING (OR JOGGING) EASY STREET

IN THIS WORLD you have easy and not-so-easy ways to make money, using Other People's Money—OPM. One of the easiest ways I know of is given you in this chapter. What is it? *It's being a finder for a fee.*

What the Finder Does for a Big Fee

Finders, as their name suggests, find things for a big fee. Let's see a few of the typical items finders might find.

- *Money* for new or not-so-new business firms needing cash.
- *Real estate* having certain characteristics—for example, a corner for a new gas station where 5000 cars pass each twenty-four hours.
- *Equipment of all kinds*—aircraft, ships, trucks, copiers, and computers, for example.
- *Brokerage houses* to take companies public. This is a very popular activity for finders in which they can earn big fees.
- *Chemicals, materials, and the like.* Finders can earn large fees finding rare chemicals and materials for companies needing them in their business.

Finding is a state of mind. You look for things, and the work just "grabs" you. Soon you transfer this approach to your own life. Before you know it, you're finding things for yourself—like OPM—and you're getting richer than you ever dreamed possible.

And another great plus for the finder is that the experience obtained can help you grow into other new careers. Here's a recent letter from a reader showing how that happened to him:

> I want to thank you for your help in getting me started in business. During a telephone conversation we had, I was looking for advice on how to get money to start investing in real estate. You suggested I contact a money broker. I did. I came away convinced that financial brokerage/finding was the business for me.
>
> I closed my first deal for a $32,000 commission. I was working with another broker in a co-broker deal and realized $16,000. I am not just a "finder" but can now provide financial consulting services, loan guarantees, and preparation of business and venture capital plans.
>
> Thanks for your personal advice and your many books. I bought and rehabilitated my first real estate property using ideas from your book *How to Make One Million in Real Estate in Three Years Starting With No Cash.* Using the HUD 203k Program, I got one loan covering the cost of purchase and rehabilitation.

So you see, the finder *can,* and often does, grow into bigger activities with a larger income. But that training as a finder stays with you through life and makes you an unsurpassed go-getter! So let's make *you* a successful finder, plus any of the other related OPM careers you'd like to pick.

How to Get Started as a Finder

There are right ways—and wrong ways—to get started as a finder. Here are the right ways. Take these steps; they're easy and quick:

1. *Decide* what types of things you'll find. It's best to have a specialty because you'll then get to know sources better. Thus, you might decide to specialize in finding money (financial broker), finding materials (commodities broker), or finding real estate (real estate broker).

2. *Pick an office* location. You can use your home to start because your clients will rarely come to visit you. Instead, you'll contact them by mail or phone or visit on rare occasions.

3. *Have your letter paper* (called a *letterhead*) printed. Don't use the word "Finder" on your letterhead. Instead, use "Consultant," "Advisor," or some similar word. It is received better than the word "Finder." Some people also use the line: "We find (or locate) anything for a fee."

4. *Get sources of what you'll find.* You can get these sources in a number of ways. For example, as a one-year or longer subscriber to the *International Wealth Success* newsletter, you can run a free classified ad each month looking for what you'll be finding. You can also run classified ads in papers like the *Wall Street Journal* or your own large-city newspaper. Why don't the people paying you to find things run these ads? Because they're usually too busy doing their regular business to take time out to think up the ads. (You'll see the wording you might use shortly.)

Proven Ways to Find What You Need

You can take several steps to find what you need. Each can get you what you're looking for. They are

1. *Advertising for what you need.* The classified ad is best for this purpose. Although a full-page ad may seem to get more attention, the added cost really doesn't get you the return you should have, considering how much more the full-page ad costs ($2500 for a full page versus $35 for a classified ad).

2. *Talking to people*—friends, business associates, and strangers. Tell them what you're looking for. But do *not* tell them what kind of a fee you'll be paid. Because *no* license of any kind is required by any state or federal agency to be a finder, people you talk to may jump right into the business if you tell them the size of the fee you'll earn.

3. *Checking with trade associations.* Almost every product or service has a trade association that has lots of free information about the specialty. You'll find them listed in a *Directory of Trade Associations,* available in any large public library.

Now let's look at each of these ways to see how you might use it to build your fortune as a finder and how you might "graduate" to a higher level and higher paying specialty!

Use Classified Ads to Find Anything

Classified ads are short, usually twenty-five to fifty words. You pay by the word. And they're "classified" by the publication into various categories like

- Money Wanted; Money Available.
- Business Opportunities; Businesses for Sale.
- Loans by Mail; Mailing Lists.
- Moneymaking Opportunities; Financial.
- Additional Income; Agents Wanted.
- Bargains and Closeouts.

Pick the category of classified ad that best fits what you're trying to find. Let's say you're looking for $500,000 for a client for a real estate deal. The ad that you run might read

$500,000 NEEDED for real estate purchase. Excellent collateral; high interest paid. Write: ABC, 123 Main St, Anytown, U.S. Or, call 123–4567 day or night.

The first two or three words of the usual classified ad are run in all capital letters or in **boldface** letters. This way the need pops right out at the reader. That's why you should try to make your first two or three words carry most of your need. Again,

$1 MILLION WANTED for business start-up. Fast repayment; excellent interest rate. Call 123–4567.

The best way to write your classified ad is to use as many words as needed to get your idea across. Then work at cutting back the number of words to as few as possible. Because you're paying by the word, the fewer words you use, the lower the cost of your ad. Also, the shorter your ad, the faster it can be read and acted on by your reader.

To get the fastest results from classified ads, take advantage of these modern ways of doing business:

- *Use an 800 toll-free number* to get replies to ads in national publications.
- *Send information by Express Mail* to deliver papers and documents overnight. Or, use one of the courier services offering similar schedules.
- *Get a "fax" machine* where faster transmission of documents is needed. You will not need such a machine until you're a really busy finder!
- *Accept credit card charges* with electronic transmission of the charges to your bank to speed the crediting of money to your account.

Keep up with developments and try to use them in your business where they will get better results, faster. Today speed is worth money to people. They'll gladly pay extra to get the service or product sooner. And if you can deliver that speed, you'll have more customers, sooner!

Talk to People Everywhere

Don't be bashful. People are interesting and full of ideas for you. So get into the habit of talking to them. Ask questions like the following about what you're trying to find.

- Do you know of any used aircraft for sale? (You'd ask this when you're finding used aircraft for people.)
- Have you met any wealthy investors looking for new projects to invest in? (You'd ask this when you're looking for private investors for a client.)
- What new household products have you seen in your travels? (You'd ask this of a business traveler when you're looking for new household products for a client.)

Don't confine your questions to just your friends. Try business associates, then talk to strangers. Almost everyone you meet will have some information to offer you. Where should you ask your questions? Anywhere! Ask:

- At home,
- In the office,
- At parties,
- In restaurants,
- At clubs— golf, tennis, or yacht,
- On airplanes, trains, and buses.

Asking questions will give you great "people skills." You'll be able to talk to anyone without choking up or becoming timid. People are people, as they say. And you can easily get to be comfortable with anyone by talking to more people. You'll quickly find that people welcome you.

One of the biggest deals I ever worked came through talking to a stranger. Here's how it happened: When I go to meetings of business groups where I don't know too many people, I follow a routine. First, I talk to as many of the people as I know. Then, I look around for someone standing by him- or herself. I go over to that person, knowing that they're feeling lonely and unwanted, and say, "Hi, I'm Ty Hicks. I publish books and two newsletters. What do you do?" The person is usually delighted and responds with his or her name, plus career work. Then it's easy to get into an interesting conversation.

At one such meeting I was told about a group of engineers working on an important book on electronics. The person gave me the name of the lead author and where the author worked. That afternoon I got on the phone and called the author. Result? We soon had a book that went on to sell over 100,000 copies—an enormous sale for a technical book.

So don't be afraid to talk. It could mean millions to you—sooner than you think. You'll meet new people, make new friends, and get new money ideas!

Tap the Trade Associations

Trade associations are a goldmine of information for you on the field in which you're finding. And most of their information is free. Or, at least you can review the information and take notes in the trade association free of charge. For instance, if you're finding money for real estate, you should check with the local real estate association in the area where the property is located. You can get lots of information on land, financing, and lenders. One reader writes

> I just closed/brokered a commercial real estate loan for $1.8 million. Now I have my own office and my name is on the street sign for everybody to see.

You'll find the names, addresses, and phone numbers of trade associations in a directory at your public library. Pick those trade associations with whom you want to work and write them. You'll be amazed at how quickly they respond and send you plenty of free information. Use a trade association to:

- Get names of experts in the field.
- Find sources of unusual information.
- Get data on similar deals to yours.
- For any other information needs you may have that are related to your field of finding.

Refine Your Finding Work

You'll see after you earn a few finder fees that certain types of work turn you on more than others. For example:

- Money finding may appeal to you more than any other type.
- Materials, real estate, or grant finding may become "your bag."

Once you get partial to certain types of finding, you'll want to become more expert at it. Why?

- You'll become known as a "specialist finder" in the area you like.
- As such, you'll want to know everything possible about that area of work.
- Bringing you more clients and larger fees—which, after all, is the purpose of your work.

When you pick your area of specialty, you should get as much reference data about it as you can. Thus, you'll get books giving lists of people and organizations in the field, names of trade association officials who might help you by giving answers to questions, plus lists of potential clients. There are, in general, four branches of specialty in this field. They are

1. Special finder for (enter name of specialty).
2. Financial broker/consultant specializing in finding money for clients of all types.
3. Business broker specializing in finding buyers and sellers of all types of businesses.
4. Business consultant specializing in finding items and personnel for any type of business.

We've looked at the general finder. Now let's look at the other types and how you might earn your fortune on OPM doing the work of your choice. Then I'll show you how to ensure that you're paid your full fee promptly and without any disputes.

Find Money for Big Fees

Every business, large or small, needs money at one time or another. That's when business owners look to financial brokers/consultants for help. Why don't business owners go out and find the money themselves?

- Most are too busy running the business.
- Many have never raised money before and don't know where to start.
- Some are afraid of having to "beat the bushes" looking for money.

You can come to the rescue of any business and help it find money. All you have to do is

- Get from the company officials information on how much money they need and for what purpose(s).
- Decide who might provide the needed funds—a bank, commercial finance company, or venture capitalist, for example.

- Contact the potential money supplier by mail or phone and ask for the money, after supplying information about the company.

What will you earn for this work? The typical fee is 5 percent of the amount of money raised, up to $1 million. After that the fee percentage declines, as shown in Table 6.1. That table gives the famous Lehman formula, which is widely used in the field. *These fees are paid after the loan is obtained, not before.*

Never ask for nor accept "front money" or advance fees. It can only lead to trouble for you. Again, never accept or ask for front money or advance fees. It only leads to trouble!

To guarantee that you receive your agreed-on fee after you get the money for your client, use one of the agreement forms shown in Figure 6.1 after it has been approved or revised by your attorney. *Never* work without the help of a competent attorney.

What kinds of money might you find for your clients? Here are a few types with which financial brokers work:

- Loans of all types—for example, mortgages, business expansion, equipment purchase, truck and auto leasing, and start-up funding

Table 6.1 *Typical Finder Fees*

Amount of Money Raised (dollars)	Fee (%)	Your Fee (dollars)
1,000,000	5	50,000
2,000,000	4.5	90,000
3,000,000	4	120,000
4,000,000	3.5	140,000
5,000,000	3	150,000
6,000,000	2.75	165,000
7,000,000	2.5	175,000
8,000,000	2.25	180,000
9,000,000	2.10	189,000
10,000,000	2	200,000
25,000,000	1.4	350,000
50,000,000	1.2	600,000
100,000,000	1	1,000,000

It is hereby agreed that ___Your Name and Address___
will find the following items ___Name the Items(s)___
for ___Name and Address of Client___ for a fee of
___Insert Fee Amount or Percentage___ to be paid on successful
delivery of the above-named item(s). This agreement
will be valid for _____ days, after which it may be
renewed in writing by both parties. During the above-
named time, the finder, _____Your Name_____,
may identify him(her)self as representing
_____Client's Name_____ for this finding activity. This
agreement represents the full understanding between
the two parties, and no other agreements will govern
this finding. In the event that the finder delivers the
above-named item(s) to the client and they are rejected,
the finder, _____Your Name_____, will still be paid
the fee stated above. The client will pay a nonrefundable fee of $_____ to the finder as a retainer.

Agreed:

_____   _____
Your Name   Date

_____   _____
Client's Name, Title   Date

_____   _____
Witnessed—Notary   Date

Figure 6.1 *Typical Finder-Fee Agreement*

- Public or private offerings through stock brokers and
  security houses
- Government funds from federal, state, city, or county
  programs—either direct funds or funds through guaranteed loans with the guarantor being the government
  agency

- Grants for worthwhile public service-type activities by
  the firm

To find sources of funds for these and other types of
money needs, get a copy of my "Financial Broker–Finder–
Business Broker–Consultant Kit" described at the back of this
book. It provides you with more than 2000 sources of business and real estate funds.

Should you get clients or lenders first? Some people suggest getting clients first and then looking for the lenders. I
suggest that you have the lenders lined up first, as you will
with the above kit. Then when you get your first client, you
can start an immediate search for funds.

But what about expenses you may incur looking for such
funds? Should you pay for them out of your pocket? Expenses:

- Postage for letters you write and applications you send
  to possible lenders.
- Telephone calls you make to lenders and other brokers
  to find money for your client.
- Typing, copying, and similar work you do for your
  client.
- Other types of work needed to get the funds.

Costs like these can run from $100 to $250 a client. If
you have twenty clients, your costs might run from $2000 to
$5000. Should you pay these?

In my view, you should not! The client is asking you for
help and should be willing to reimburse you for any such costs
you incur because of and for the client. And the best way to
ensure that you work on OPM is to have the client advance
you the estimated amount of money you'll need on a nonrefundable basis. Here's how to work this so everyone—the client, yourself, and the lender—is happy:

1. *Estimate* the cost of finding money for the client with
   whom you're dealing.
2. *Prepare* a written agreement, such as that shown in
   Figure 6.1, covering your estimated costs.
3. *Sign the agreement* and have your client sign the
   agreement in the space provided.

4. *Keep an exact record* of every stamp, every phone call, and every other type of contact you make for the client. Make a record of the time and date of all these contracts.

By using this approach, you won't have problems whether you do or do not get funding for your client. If you do get funding you may want to, as a gesture of appreciation, return the money advanced to you. Why? The fee you get for finding the money, which is also covered by the agreement in Figure 6.1, will be several times your retainer!

Be a Business Broker and Prosper

If finding money doesn't turn you on, then perhaps you should be a business broker. This is "fun" since you get to meet lots of people in your area, you learn a great deal about businesses for sale, and you may be able to grab an opportunity for yourself because you have early information on good deals.

As a business broker people will come to you to either sell or buy a business. Most deals start with people seeking to sell a business. Then all you need do is find a buyer. This can be easy because all your looking will be through classified ads in local or national newspapers.

For finding a suitable buyer, you'll be paid a fee based on the selling price of the business. This fee can range from 5 to 10 percent of the sales price, depending on local customs and rules. Your fee is paid to you by the seller at the closing (also called *passing*) of the sale.

The typical agreement form used to ensure that you're paid your fee for finding a buyer for a business is shown in Figure 6.2. You should have your attorney prepare a suitable agreement for your area.

You'll often find that if you work as a business broker, your client will ask you to find money for a deal. Thus, you'll be asked to be a financial broker also! And the same is true when you're a financial broker. Your client may ask you to

It is hereby agreed that <u>Your Name and Address</u> will seek to sell the business known as <u>Enter Name and Address</u> for a price of no less than $_____ with a cash down payment of no less than $_____. A fee of <u>Enter Fee Amount or Percentage</u> will be paid to <u>Your Name</u> on successful completion of the sale at the closing. If <u>Your Name</u> should find a willing buyer at the price named above, or higher, and the client rejects the buyer for any reason, <u>Your Name</u> will be paid the full commission agreed on above.

This agreement represents the full understanding between the two parties, and no other agreement will govern this sale. <u>Your Name</u> will have exclusive right to this sale for _____ days. A nonrefundable retainer of $_____ will be paid to <u>Your Name</u> on the signing of this agreement.

Agreed:

_____	_____
Your Name	Date
_____	_____
Client's Name, Title	Date
_____	_____
Witnessed—Notary	Date

Figure 6.2 *Typical Business Broker Sales Agreement*

find a buyer for a division or part of the company that he or she wants to sell. So you're made a business broker, overnight!

To make big money as a business broker:

- Get a number of businesses to sell.
- Don't depend on selling just one business a week or a month.

- Profits in this business really build up when you have a dozen or so businesses to offer.

Specialize, if you wish. Most business brokers, however, handle a wide range of sales because they make more money this way. Keep a good attorney and accountant "on tap"— you'll need both in your buying and selling work. See the "Financial Broker–Finder–Business Broker–Consultant Kit" listed at the back of this book for more information on getting rich on OPM as a business broker.

Consult and Find for Any Business

You can become a business consultant on OPM if you have a wide background in general business. Or, you can also become a consultant if you have a narrow specialty in a certain field. Either way you can make big bucks— from $500 to $5000 a day, plus expenses—depending on your specialty and reputation.

What's the easiest way for you to get started as a business consultant? Here are the simple steps to take:

1. *Decide* what your specialty will be. You *must* be an expert in your specialty.
2. *Get publicity* for your availability as a consultant by sending news releases to your local papers and magazines. Do the same with national publications in your field. Figure 6.3 shows a typical consultant's news release, which gets fast results.
3. *Have your business letterheads* and calling cards printed. Don't go overboard with colors or fancy designs. A simple, black-and-white format that's completely businesslike is best.
4. *Write* letters to local businesses that might use your specialty. Enclose copies of your news release.
5. *Offer* lower prices to your first few clients. This will give you names of clients you can use for creditability purposes in getting new clients.
6. *Keep* expanding your practice, getting as many clients as you can handle. Most consultants work four days

News Release—For Immediate Release

_____Your Name_____ announces the opening of
his (her) business consulting agency to be located at
_____Your Address_____, telephone
number _____. _____Your Name_____ is an
experienced business and financial consultant, having
worked with a number of firms in both the local and
national areas.

Consulting assignments _____Your Name_____
will accept include raising capital, finding buyers and
sellers for businessess, improving profits of existing
businesses, researching new products, developing new
personnel for existing or new positions, plus many
other assignments. _____Your Name_____ will work
on either a per-diem basis or a flat-fee annual retainer
covering a specified number of consulting days per
year. Clients can arrange to use either plan, depending
on their needs.

Numerous local and national firms have already
expressed interest in using the services of the new
consulting agency. _____Your Name_____ can be
reached by telephone at _____, or in writing at
_____Your Address_____.

Figure 6.3   _Typical News Release Announcing Formation of_
a Business Consulting Firm

with clients and use the fifth day to "ventilate their
schedules"—that is, catch up on reading, rest their
minds, and think about the jobs they did during the
week.

Many of my readers are consultants today. How did they
become consultants? This is what one reader told me on the
phone:

Ty, I became a financial broker because I wanted to get close to the sources of money in my area. Inside of six months I really knew who was lending for what use and which kinds of deals they liked. I became an expert on loans for business and real estate. Soon my clients were asking me questions about how they should run their businesses to earn more money. And I was surprised to learn that somehow I had picked up information that was valuable to these clients. They were willing to pay me for talking and for later putting my thoughts on paper. Before I knew it, I was talking to my clients about a lot more than just loans. So today I'm a full-fledged consultant at $1000 a day, plus expenses. It really beats working for a living!

One other aspect that I've noticed about businesspeople might make you smile. But it can also put money into your pocket, using OPM. This aspect is:

- That there seems to be an inherent respect for the person who has or can get money for business or real estate. Clients tend to think of such a person as all knowing. So they look to the financial broker to solve all other business problems—almost all of which come back to money anyway! You *can* make a fortune walking easy street.

Protect Your Fees With Good Agreements

You will always be paid by a satisfied client if you have a properly worded written agreement covering your services and fees. The key to getting paid by any client is to have a written agreement with the client. Starting this very moment, resolve:

- *Not to work* on the basis of a friendly handshake; they're quickly forgotten by everyone but you.
- *Not to work* for love, friendship, good fellowship, or any other nonmonetary reason and expect to be paid. You can, of course, work for any of these reasons if you want to be charitable. But don't expect to be paid.
- *Not to work* for a client who says, "Oh, I'll get to the agreement next week and send it to you. Meanwhile,

though, could you kindly help us with these problems we have right now?" *Never* start work until you have the written, signed agreement in hand if you expect to be paid.

We've given you two examples of typical agreements in this chapter. If you want other examples, see the "Financial Broker–Finder–Business Broker–Consultant Kit" listed at the back of this book. It gives you dozens and dozens of other examples of tried, tested, and proven agreements for this great business.

Of course, you should *never* use a sample agreement without first having it approved by your attorney. Although this may seem a nuisance, you will be well repaid if you consult your attorney whenever you're using a written agreement of any kind. Take time *before* signing an agreement to determine if the document is fair, precise, and legal.

Get the License Question Answered Early

Almost everyone considering finding as a business to make money on OPM eventually asks, "Do I need a license to be a finder?" Here's the answer in both general and specific terms:

- A finder who introduces two people just for the purpose of having them arrange a deal and who then steps out of the picture and does not participate in the deal in any other way, except to be paid an agreed-on fee, *never need be licensed.*

This view has been expressed in courts of law in many different states over the years. *You do not have to be licensed to introduce two or more people.* It's only when you begin to handle papers, draw up agreements, and so on, that the question of a license comes up. Let's take a closer look.

You *must* have a valid license to engage in certain regulated activities in every state. Thus,

- You must be a licensed real estate broker to engage in regulated real estate transactions.

- You must be a licensed attorney to give legal advice for a fee, represent clients, and the like.

These are the only two professions for which a license requiring an examination is required (omitting engineers, accountants, and physicians, for example, who do not work actively in this field).

As an example, in certain states a "commission broker's license" is required. But to get such a license you simply fill out an application, bring it to the local state office, pay a small fee, and walk away with your license. And even where a license that would take long study and a tough exam is required, BWBs have found legal ways to comply with the law. For example

- In real estate deals, finders will hire a real estate professional for a fee to handle the needed work for them.
- Other finders will act as consultants to licensed specialists, assisting them in the deal.
- Still other finders unite with retired licensed personnel, bringing them deals on which to work.

The whole key here with respect to licenses is:

- Smart BWBs wanting to make a fortune on OPM without having to go through the steps of getting a license often associate themselves with licensed personnel for one or more deals so that every step of the transaction is fully in accord with the laws governing it.

You *must* act completely within the law! *Never* break the law for any amount of money. The reward is never worth the possible penalties you might incur.

Licenses are *not* required for a number of the activities we're discussing. Namely:

- Finders and consultants never need licenses.
- Financial brokers and business brokers rarely need a license.

But the only way for you to find out the exact law in your area is to consult an attorney. Ask the attorney to research the law and its loopholes. Why?

- Almost every law written has one or more loopholes.
- It may be possible for you to operate inside the loop-holes without a license.
- Meaning that you can build wealth on OPM as a financial broker–finder–business broker–consultant.

Grab the Big Money Available for Finders

Almost every business needs a finder at one time or another. And *you* can provide most businesses with the services that they require. Your fee income can be significant because:

- You can start with less than a $100 investment.
- You work on OPM because it pays for your time and expenses.
- Experience as a finder can lead to better-paying consulting activities.
- You'll make many valuable contacts with important people when you work as a finder.

Yes, there still *is* an easy street to wealth on OPM. And it's full of fun and interesting people, stimulating ideas, and great conversation! That street? It's the finder's world—one you can work in full-time, part-time, or even just once a year.

This chapter gives you the basics. Start *now* to put the ideas here to work in your life. You'll be delighted with the results. And if you ever have a question on a deal, an agreement, or a fee, I'm as close to you as your telephone!

CHAPTER 7

USE A GOLDEN TOUCH TO GET MONEY WITHOUT STRINGS

You CAN GET MONEY for worthwhile purposes that need *never* be repaid. You might call this the ultimate use of OPM: purposes that benefit people. Just what kind of money am I talking about?

I'm talking about *grants.* A grant is money advanced to your organization to perform some worthwhile service for people and/or communities. Thus, grants might be made to:

- *Study* health patterns in a given area of the country.
- *Restore* an historic building important to national or state history.
- *Analyze* traffic patterns on a given highway or freeway system.
- *Provide* cultural entertainment during certain periods of the year.

Thousands of grants are made every year for such purposes. Why shouldn't you and your organization get one of these grants, if you wish to? Let's see how you might get some of this "free money," starting right now.

Who Makes Grants?

Grants are made by many different types of organizations. Here's a list of the most frequent grant makers (called *grantors*):

- United States Government through its various agencies and departments
- State governments
- City and county governments
- Corporations of medium and large size
- Foundations of many types

Many billions of dollars are given out in grants every year. The purpose of these grants is to help the health, education, cultural, historical, and community well-being in both national and local areas. If you can perform one of these tasks, you and your organization have a good chance of getting a grant.

For What Purposes Are Grants Made?

Grants are made to help people or communities. Grants are *not* made to earn a profit for you or your organization. Grants:

- Reimburse you and your firm for work done.
- Cover expenses like salary costs, rent, light, heat, and other utilities.
- Along with supplies, travel, research, and the like.

Any grant money you receive is to pay for estimated expenses you'll have in accomplishing the purpose of the grant. *No* allowance is made for profit. Organizations making grants don't advance money for profits—they only pay out for expected costs related to the purpose of the grant. But don't turn away from grants thinking that they're a waste of time. Grants can get you many beneficial results, as we'll see later.

The most common purposes for which grants are made include

- Improvement of health of the general public.
- Restoration of historic structures and areas.
- Scientific research of many different kinds related to defense and national well-being.
- Encouragement of the arts—music, literature, and theatre, for example.

- Building or expanding health and social care facilities (hospitals and homes for the aged).
- Improving public facilities such as transportation, highway, railroad, and airline.
- Increasing safety for workers and the general public.

Then there are "favorites" in the areas of grants. Such favorites are grants made by foundations set up for highly specialized purposes. Examples of such grants might be for the

- Study of the feeding habits of polar bears.
- Analysis of workloads in the garment industry.
- Improvement of cockpit crew coordination in commercial aircraft.

Why might favorites be important to you? Because one of the favorites might tie in exactly with the type of work you and your firm are capable of doing. You might be the only person in your state, or in the entire country, capable of doing the work for a favored grant subject!

What Types of Grants Should You Seek?

You should *not* "go off the handle" and apply for every grant in sight just because it offers a chance for free money. Instead, you should

1. *Analyze* your interests and the capability of your organization.
2. *Decide* what types of grants would be best handled by your firm.
3. *Assemble* information on your capabilities—such as staff, education, and experience.
4. *Choose* "target" grantors who are interested in the type of grant work you plan to do.
5. *Develop* a plan for getting the grant(s) you seek, being certain you can do outstanding work.

To do your best work on a grant assignment, you or your staff should have extensive experience in the field in which you'll work. Some education in the field will also lend greater creditability to your application and efforts. The key is:

- Don't try to "wing it" when applying for grant money.
  Instead, look around until you find a grantor making
  grants for the type of work you like and do well. Why?
  One grant that's successfully accomplished can lead to
  others with much less work in the application process.
  So go for what you (or your staff) know; do the best job
  you can; finish it *on* schedule and *on* budget.

There's plenty of money for you in grants. But you must
approach them with a complete *business attitude*. Any other
view of grants wastes your time!

Where Do You Find Grantors?

Grantors, as you'll recall, *make* grants (give out money).
You, as the receiver of this money, are the *grantee*. These two
words save time and space in explaining what you can do to
get some of this free money.

Grantors are easy to find. Just do some local research in
your library, and you'll come up with hundreds (or even thousands) of names and addresses of grantors. Look at these
sources:

- Directories of foundations—there are many available
  that list foundations throughout the country.
- Corporation directories list those corporations that
  make grants for various purposes.
- Federal government data lists thousands of grants that
  are available.
- State, city, and county directories list grants that you
  can get.
- The "Yellow Pages" of your local large-city telephone
  book lists them under the entry "Foundations."

In helping BWBs get grants—the ultimate OPM—we
prepared our grants kit, called "Raising Money From Grants
and Other Sources." It includes a directory listing more than
25,000 foundations. You'll find details on this kit at the back
of this book.

Like any other search effort, you *must* use your head and
your ingenuity when looking for grantors. Sometimes you'll

find that you're the only applicant a grantor has been approached by in years. Why? Because other people have not
"done their homework" in looking for a grantor. If you do
your homework, you'll be surprised at the amount of OPM
you can tap!

How to Apply for a Grant

There are specific steps to take to apply for a grant. Don't
try to shortcut these steps. Why? In the field of grants — sometimes called *grantsmanship* — a two-page single-spaced letter
may get you several hundred thousand dollars in grants. So
why try to take shortcuts when the amount of work to get
started is so little? The steps that are winners with people seeking grants of all kinds are as follows:

1. *Obtain* your tax-exempt status from the Internal Rev-
   enue Service (IRS) to get foundation grants.
2. *Decide* what types of grants you'll apply for. Without
   knowing what types of grants you seek, your efforts
   will be wasted.
3. *Target* your potential grantors. Go for numbers here.
   The more grantors the better your chances of getting
   the grant you seek.
4. *Prepare* your grant proposal. Be clear, be concise, and
   be accurate.
5. *Submit* your proposal to the grantors you've chosen as
   "targets."
6. *Wait* for a positive response. If you're turned down,
   keep trying.
7. *Do the grant work,* if you're approved. Be certain to
   deliver *more* than you promised. Then you'll be set to
   get a second grant.

Don't let these steps frighten you; they are simple. Some people can prepare a grant proposal in just a few hours. The
hourly "pay" for doing the proposal can be enormous, especially when you're aiming at big bucks!

Let's take a look at each of these steps and see how it's
done. You'll see that getting grants is much easier than you
might think.

Obtain Your Tax-Exempt Status

If you plan to get grants from foundations—and there are more than 30,000 in the United States alone—you *must* be a tax-exempt organization. You can easily get this status—*free*—from the IRS by filling out an easy-to-understand form.

Just call your local IRS office and ask for a copy of the tax-exempt form; they'll send it to you. Fill it out answering all the questions that apply to you, and send it in. After about six weeks you should have your response. If your request is approved, you'll be given a tax-exempt number. Use this on all your proposals and correspondence with foundations. It's hard to get grants from foundations if you don't have your tax-exempt status. Don't let this requirement "throw you." It's easy to satisfy. You don't have to pay any money, and approval is reasonably fast. And you can, of course, go on applying for grants from corporations, governments, and other grantors where tax-exempt status is not required.

Decide What Types of Grants You'll Apply For

As was said earlier, you *must* know something about the field in which you're applying for grants. Thus, let's say you're applying for a grant to teach local high school students the Civil War history of the Flashing River area of the state. To get a grant for this purpose, you *must:*

- Know something about Civil War history in general.
- Know local Civil War history in the Flashing River area of the state.
- Know the basics of teaching people in history.

Of course, you *can* have a staff of history teachers who will do the teaching for you. But to prepare the proposal you *do* need to know something about Civil War history. You probably wouldn't even pick such a topic for your grant if you didn't know anything about this period of history.

You can, if you wish, hire people and then "wrap a grant proposal around them." Thus, if you know a little about science and you detect a growing need for certain scientific research, you can hire capable science people and get them to prepare your proposal. The only drawback is that your staff may leave you after the grant work is done because they see how easy it is to get a grant with the right staff.

If you're an expert in some area of information, you can almost certainly get a grant on your own. All you need do is find a grantor that wants your type of expertise to fund a study or activity. Write your proposal (or have someone write it for you) and send it to the grantors you've picked. A good proposal is almost certain to get the funds you seek. To summarize:

- Know the field in which you want to work.
- Get to know the grantors in this field.
- Tailor your proposal to your grantors.
- Keep applying until you get your grant.

Target Your Potential Grantors

In the "Phone-In/Mail-In Grants Kit" listed at the back of this book, I recommend that you target your potential grantors by:

- *Phoning* to find if the grant you seek is of interest to the grantor.
- *Writing* the grantor, asking the same questions.
- *Saving time* for yourself and the grantor because you won't send unwanted proposals.

By using the phone-in/mail-in technique, you can find dozens of *interested* grantors in a day or so. Once you've found them, you can concentrate on getting the grant money you seek from one or more of these grantors.

So don't waste anyone's time. Go right to the target! Find out if the work you're proposing to do under a grant is really wanted by any grantors. There's *no* sense trying to make a grantor want to do the work that interests you. It is better to do the work the grantor is interested in doing. That's where the money is and where it will continue to be.

Prepare Your Grant Proposal

Many BWBs seeking OPM through grants think that a proposal must be six inches thick to win a grant. Not so! When questioned, most people in charge of approving grants say

- The shorter the proposal, the faster its approval.
- Short proposals are read first, long proposals last.
- A two-page proposal letter is enough to get a tentative "Yes" answer.
- Grantees who save grantor's time are always popular and they're remembered.
- Long proposals don't convince as strongly as short proposals do.

So recognize, here and now, that conciseness pays off! Make your proposal short, and you may win those big-buck grants sooner. Since you can get a quick answer on the possibility of getting a specific grant that interests you with just one phone call or a short letter:

- Prepare your proposal in summary form to start.
- Use this summary as your letter or phone script.
- Get a quick answer first.
- Then expand your proposal to include more data.

To show what I mean, let's say you've decided to apply for a grant as detailed earlier to teach high school students Civil War history for your area. Your summary proposal might read like this:

> We seek a $150,000 grant to teach 1500 local high school students the history of the Civil War in the Flashing River area of the state. Included will be tours of battlefields, visits to local museums, and lectures on the heroes of the battles.

Once you get a grantor interested in making this grant, you can fill in the other topics of your proposal, namely,

- The need—why the grant work is needed.
- What will be done—a description of the work you'll do.
- Who will do the work—information on your staff.

- How results will be measured—tests or other measures you'll use.
- How much money is needed and how it will be used.
- The future—what other grants might be used to continue this work.

You have your targeted grantors, and you now have a brief outline of your proposal. Your next step is to call or write all target grantors, asking if they're interested. If you call targeted grantors, you'll get faster answers. Don't be afraid to call! Grantors *need* your business to stay in business. If you call, use this wording:

> Good morning (or afternoon). We're seeking a $150,000 grant to teach Civil War history to local high school students in the state, especially those in the Flashing River area. The grant will be for one year. Would you (or your organization) be interested in making such a grant?

You'll get an immediate "Yes" or "No" answer. If the answer is "Yes," say "Would a two-page proposal be enough for you to make your decision?" The answer to this question will probably be "Yes." If it is, say "Thanks. We'll get the proposal to you within the next three days. To whom should I address it?" Make notes of *everything* you're told, including the name of the person to whom you're told to send your proposal. When you first ask your question about the grant and if the answer is "No," say "What kinds of grants *are* you making today? For what typical amounts?" Jot down the answer! Why? You may be able to qualify for one of the grants the organization *is* making. So your phone call won't be wasted. If you'd rather write to grantors to learn if they'd be interested in your grant request, use a short letter like that shown in Figure 7.1. Call in advance to get the name of the person to whom you should address your letter.

Finish Your Proposal Sections. Your proposal will have six *brief* sections, following the initial statement covering the grant amount and time period, along with the purpose of the grant. This information is in the first paragraph of the letter in Figure 7.1. This will be followed by the six sections, thus:

Date

_____

_____

Dear _____ :

We are seeking a grant of $150,000 for one year to teach Civil War history to high school students in the Flashing River area of the State of _____ .

Your organization has been chosen as a possible grantor.

Those who would benefit from this grant include the high school students, their teachers, their parents, members of local government, and state historical societies.

We look forward to your response concerning your interest in this grant request. A full proposal is available if the grant request interests you.

Very truly yours,

Figure 7.1   *Typical Grant Request Letter*

- *The Need:* High school students in the Flashing River area are not familiar with the rich Civil War history associated with the area. Ignorance of the important events in the area leaves these students at a disadvantage in their lives. Further, the area suffers because its residents are not as well informed as they should be.
- *What Will Be Done:* This grant will furnish funds to teach these students about the important Civil War

events that took place in the Flashing River area. Guided tours to battlefields, museums, and other historic
sites will be part of the teaching strategy. The grant
will provide teaching facilities for 1500 local students.
The program will supplement the students' regular
history courses, which do not give enough attention to
local history.

- *Who Will Do the Work:* A staff of four competent histo-
rians will conduct the studies on a part-time basis, including the tours and lectures on-site. This staff will
impart a genuine feeling of important history to every
student in the program.

- *Measuring Results:* Students will be tested at two-week
intervals to determine their comprehension and understanding of the topics presented. The grantor will
be sent the results of these tests at two-week intervals.
A final examination will rate each student on his or her
understanding of the history of the area.

- *Money Needed:* A total of $150,000 is needed for one
year to cover salaries, office expenses, travel, group
transportation, and miscellaneous costs. Detailed
breakdowns of each expense category are available and
will be sent to the grantor on request.

- *The Future:* If this program is successful, as the grantee expects it will be, future high school classes can be
taught in the same way. Further, other areas of the
state can be served with similar programs.

That's it. The above simple proposal could get you $150,000
for one year to do the work described. And if the grantor likes
the work you do, you may get many other grants from the
same organization!

Take the Grants Road to OPM

Grants help people. You can help people by getting
grants for work that's important in your area or in the nation.
You'll get a good feeling from doing this. But what's more important, you will benefit in many ways by getting and working
on grants. These ways include the following:

- You'll learn how to manage people.
- You will become a known figure in your bank because you'll deposit grant funds and write checks.
- People will look up to you when they learn that you're doing important work for humanity or for your community.
- You'll meet important people in the area—people who may later help you in profit-making work.
- You will become an expert in putting together business proposals and plans, all of which can benefit you enormously in the future in your own business.
- You'll have operating funds in the meanwhile for your grants work—perhaps more than you've ever seen in one check at one time.

So if you can do something for people or for an area or if you can get people who can do this, consider grants. They could be your first step to great riches on OPM—your route going from flat broke to great wealth!

CHAPTER 8

STRIKE IT RICH GROWING BIG FORTUNES FROM SMALL SEEDS

THE MOST EXCITING development in using OPM is risk capital, better known as venture capital. This form of OPM has built more fortunes in the last few years than any other type of funding. And you can make money from venture capital in a number of different ways. If you're turned on by new ventures, if getting funds for yourself or others excites you, if great wealth just "grabs you," then venture capital is the way to go! Let's see how.

Understand Venture Capital Now

Venture capital is money put into a company to help that company grow, while so, too, does the money. A firm must be a corporation to obtain venture capital. Why? Venture capitalists put money into a firm by buying some shares of stock in the corporation. This kind of money is called *equity capital* because the venture capitalist is buying part of ownership or "equity" in the firm.

Venture capitalists hope to see their money grow by at least five times in five years or less. Let's see how this might work. Say that a venture capitalist:

- Buys 100,000 shares of stock in a new (start-up) company for $10 a share, or $1 million.
- Your company, if you own it, gets the $1 million to use in the business.

129

- You and the venture capitalist hope that your business improves to a level where your stock is worth $60 or more a share.
- When the stock value reaches that level, the venture capitalist may elect to sell out, getting $6 million for the stock. This means that the venture capitalist earned a profit of $6 million − $1 million invested = $5 million.

The venture capitalist, of course, takes a risk. Your business might not grow as fast as expected. Or, it may run into problems and require more cash to give the desired growth. Worse yet, the business may not make the expected earnings and will have to be shut down. The venture capitalist might lose every penny invested.

You can't be hurt if you're on the receiving end of venture capital. Why? You don't have any debts to repay. Venture capital is *risk capital;* you do *not* have to sign a loan application, pledge personal assets, and so on. So venture capital can be the dream road to wealth on OPM!

Ways You Can Make Money From Venture Capital

There are a number of different ways to make money from OPM venture capital. Pick one or more for your future fortune:

- *Raise venture capital* for your own firm by getting money from a venture capitalist.
- *Form a venture capital fund* and get money from investors to put into new and growing firms as a venture capitalist.
- *Help firms get venture capital* by looking over their businesses and deciding which venture capitalist might help them. You earn a fee for finding the venture money for the firm.
- *Organize a venture capital club* in your area and hold meetings for firms seeking money. Charge a nominal but profitable fee for the lunch or breakfast meeting, depending on the time of day you hold the get-together.

- *Prepare venture capital Executive Summary write-ups* and/or business plans for a fee. This gives you good experience and can lead to important earnings for you.

You may come upon other ways to earn money from venture capital deals as you work in this great field. For example, my corporate attorney recently told me about a mutual friend who's a venture capitalist:

> Once I did some work for John (not his real name), and he offered to pay me with shares of stock in a firm for which he supplied venture capital. I really wanted a check for my fee but John urged me to take the stock. I did and today that stock has "gone through the roof." It gave me the best fee income I've ever earned in my life! I wish I had a few more like that one.

Thus, you might take part of your fee for work you do getting venture capital for others as a share in the company being financed. If the firm booms, as some do, you could be wealthy. Just think of the great success stories in recent years—Apple Computer, Compaq Computer, and Federal Express—and you'll realize how a company can grow from one employee to thousands in a few years. And sales and profits can often match employee growth. That's where you cash in—when you sell stock that cost you almost nothing!

How to Raise Money From Venture Capitalists

In the lingo of venture capitalists, there are just two kinds of deals into which they'll put money:

- High tech.
- Low tech.

High tech (meaning high-level technology) is represented by companies in businesses that use lots of technology such as computers, solid-state electronics, advanced material sciences, and medical technology. Such firms are said to be on the cutting edge of technology. And no matter what venture capitalists may say, they *do* like high-tech ventures!

Low tech (meaning low-level technology) is represented

by firms in more traditional businesses—ones that have been known for years—such as retailing (selling to consumers— you and me), services of all kinds (repairs, cleaning, health maintenance), and other matter-of-fact businesses.

In recent years, venture capitalists have turned more to low-tech ventures because the possibility of new high-tech ventures dried up. And their experience with low-tech ventures has been good. So most venture capitalists today are glad to look at both types of deals.

To raise money from a venture capitalist, you must take several proven steps. These steps are as follows:

1. *Decide* if the venture for which you want to raise venture capital is high tech or low tech.
2. *Prepare* (or have someone in the firm prepare) an Executive Summary detailing in four or fewer short paragraphs what the firm does, which markets it serves, what staff capabilities the firm has, how much money is needed, and what profits are expected when the money is put to work. This Executive Summary should be typed single-spaced on one sheet of paper.
3. *Choose* four or more venture capitalists whom you think might be interested in the type of project you're handling. Note that this project may be your own firm. Or, it might be a project for another firm for whom you're trying to raise money for a fee. Either way, you proceed in a similar manner.
4. *Send* the Executive Summary to the venture capital firms you chose in step 3. Enclose a letter stating that a copy of the full business plan is available, if desired. (A sample of this letter is given later.)
5. *Provide* the business plan, if requested. You'll learn later in this chapter how to prepare the business plan or supervise its preparation.
6. *Collect* the venture capital and put it to work as detailed in the Executive Summary.

What Turns On Venture Capitalists

Venture capitalists see hundreds of business proposals every month. Yet just a few "turn them on." Why?

- Because very few business proposals are well prepared.
- Most proposals fail to give key information.
- Few proposals recognize what the venture firm seeks.

If you know the "hot button" that turns on venture capitalists, you can get deals funded faster and with much less hassle. Here's what turns on most venture capitalists to the point where they're ready to put money into your deal:

- Unique business ideas with large profit potential
- Special protection for an idea—a patent or copyright, for example
- Aggressive management dedicated to making the business tops in its field
- Experienced management that knows how to run a company and make it successful
- Clearly stated company and financial goals

Knowing these turn-ons, you'll want to reflect them in your Executive Summary. Why is this so important?

- With hundreds of proposals coming in every month, you want yours to "star" and get read.
- The Executive Summary should be able to be read in less than a minute. If it "grabs" the venture capitalist, the entire business plan will be requested.
- So have your Executive Summary present the desired information quickly and easily!

Today some firms are going high tech with venture capital requests. The firm and its staff are put on videotape. The tape is sent to the venture firm along with an Executive Summary. But the tape isn't viewed unless the Executive Summary pushes that hot button. So you really rise or fall based on the Executive Summary.

To show you what kind of an Executive Summary can get money for firms, Figures 8.1 and 8.2 give actual summaries recently sent to venture capital firms. Note that each is neat, concise, and to the point. Neither summary makes wild claims. The letter accompanying such a summary is shown in Figure 8.3. You can use it as is or change it to suit your needs.

If you use the "Venture Capital Millions Kit," described

Executive Summary

_____, Inc., needs $400,000 venture capital to install five (5) shower trailers at truck-stop locations around the United States. These shower trailers will provide truck drivers with the opportunity to take showers in clean, neat, and well-maintained facilities. Today there are few truck stops anywhere that provide such facilities for truckers.

Statistics show that some 8000 truckers go to the East Coast of the United States every day. Many of these truckers require shower facilities after being on the road hour after hour. _____, Inc., will provide these facilities in specially manufactured trailers installed at key truck stops.

For the first year, _____, Inc., projects significant revenues and profits from four profit centers, namely:

PROFIT CENTER NO.	ACTIVITY	PROJECTED PROFIT, $
1	Five company-owned shower trailers at five sites	567,000
2	Trailer manufacturing	120,000
3	Franchise sales	240,000
4	Franchise royalties	75,000
	TOTAL	1,002,000

The totals shown here are just for the full six (6) months' operation during the first year of the business. Future years will show higher profits for the company. Management projects that the company will be worth $10 million in less than five years.

The company, _____, Inc., is headed by a young, experienced management graduate who has extensive trucking, construction, and mining experience. He is qualified to build the shower trailers. His trucking experience has shown him those areas of the country that would be most profitable for shower trailers.

This company offers a needed service with a specially built product that will be welcomed by almost every truck stop in the country. Any investor will be well rewarded by the growth in the company's value over the years.

Full information on the company can be obtained from _____ Associates, P.O. Box 1234, Anytown, Anystate 12345.

Figure 8.1   *Example of a Typical Executive Summary*

Executive Summary

_____ Enterprises, Inc., seeks $3 million in venture capital to fund construction and inventory for a proprietary videotape-rental system targeted for the convenience food store market. A number of convenience stores have expressed strong interest in immediate installation of the system in multiple outlets.

The "Convenience Video" (CV) unit is simple and trouble free. Certain key features are proprietary, along with the controlling computer programs. Manufacturing costs are low, and components are readily available. Central to the CV network of units is the CV data center. Use of modern software and communication techniques permits management of units anywhere there are telephones. Units also work if communication is lost or not available.

An experienced management team is in place. Personnel with marketing, manufacturing, and business experience in computer science are on board.

Sales and marketing objectives promise significant profits for all investors. Attached financial projections include eventual sale of stock to the public to repay initial investments.

The many advantages offered by the CV system make it a potential leader in this important consumer field. Investors will be rewarded with growth far beyond that normally experienced in consumer projects.

Full information on this interesting and profitable opportunity is available from _____ Enterprises, Inc.,
_____
Address

Attn. _____, President.

Figure 8.2   *Another Example of an Executive Summary*

at the back of this book, I will personally prepare an Executive Summary for you based on nonconfidential data you supply me. Also, I'll recommend three or more venture capitalists who might fund your deal. Of course, there's *no* guarantee that the venture funds will be put up if I prepare the Executive Summary. But you will know that a professional prepared the summary. And if the information is such that I don't think you can get venture funds, I'll tell you so. And I'll also tell you how you might revise the data to possibly get venture money.

Sure Turn-Downs You Should Avoid

Venture capitalists *are* looking for certain features in the firms they fund. Here are some reasons they will *not* fund:

- Amounts less than $500,000—it costs just as much to process a $100,000 deal as a $1 million one.
- One-person companies— venture capitalists like depth in numbers of people. You should have at least two people.
- Slow-growth businesses that have little future such as coin laundries or dry-cleaning stores.
- Unique special-skills businesses (such as artists, sculptors, poets, or writers) where the output depends on just one person's skills.
- Fundings that traditionally are funded by loans; thus, a long-term real estate mortgage is a loan, not venture capital.

Venture capitalists seek to put their money into businesses that will have these characteristics:

- Fast growth.
- Competitive advantages.
- Unique products or services.
- Strong management.
- Drive for success.
- "Right" numbers (see above).

You *can* get venture funds for yourself or others. It all depends on having the right deal, well-presented. As a reader writes, "I'm about to close on a venture capital deal for $4 million. Then I hope to go full-time as a full-service financial broker."

Now let's move on to the next step in getting venture capital for yourself or others. You'll see how to have a business plan that wins money for the business seeking it!

Prepare a Winning Business Plan

Preparing a business plan for your own business can be the best mind-clearing work you'll ever do. Why?

- A business plan tells you where you're headed with your business.
- Shows what financing, equipment, and people you'll need to reach your goals.
- Gives you a "feel" for whether your proposed business can really succeed.

It's for all these reasons that venture capitalists insist on seeing a business plan *before* funding any deal. Yet a business plan that runs just twenty pages or so can get you millions of investment capital. So the time you spend doing your plan can pay out at thousands of dollars an hour!

And if you're seeking other kinds of funds from banks, the federal or state government, or private investors, a business plan can get you your money faster and with less explaining on your part. So don't shirk doing a business plan or having someone prepare one for you.

A reader who specializes in helping small businesses raise money with well-prepared business plans writes:

> You'll be pleased to know that I helped my small-business clients raise almost exactly $2 million in the last twelve months. Methods I learned from your books and courses were responsible for most of that success. In the next twelve months I expect to double that amount.

So business plans *do* work for you and your clients. Let's now see how you can prepare or supervise the preparation of a good business plan.

Items to Include in Your Business Plan

Every business plan covers certain key items venture capitalists look for. These items are

- The Executive Summary — very important (see above).
- The business — what it is, why you (or your client) want to go into it and the advantages of your approach to the business over the competition.
- Financial and position goals — what profits you seek for the company in three years, five years; where the company will be positioned with respect to the competition in the same periods.
- Products or services offered — what they are and why they should beat the competition.
- Your market — how many people, companies, or other buying or using units exist, where they are, and what they're willing to pay for what you'll offer them.
- Competition — who they are, what they sell, which advantages they have, what their drawbacks are, and how you plan to outsell competitors.
- Use of proceeds — how you'll use the money the venture capitalist provides.
- Marketing strategies that will maximize use of the proceeds and outsell the competition.
- Management — who they are, what experience they have, and where they'll take the company.
- Description of offer — what the venture capitalist will buy in terms of the stock in the corporation when money is invested. You should have a competent attorney assist you with this section.
- Pro forma (meaning *provided in advance*) financial statements showing the firm's expected income, expenses, and profits for the first three years. These statements should be prepared on a month-to-month basis so trends are easy to see.
- Warnings to investors — if your company (or client's) is a new one, be sure to point out the risks the investors face. Tell what might (or could) go wrong. Don't be afraid of scaring venture capitalists! They've seen all this before and know what risks every new business faces. Tell it as it is, and your chances of getting big bucks are much, much greater than if you try to deny what everyone knows: business is risk-taking.

Although I'd certainly like to show you a typical, winning business plan, we don't have enough space in this book. But if you use the "Business Plan Kit" described at the back of this book, you'll get an excellent example of a successful business plan. Also, you receive full instructions on how to write your own business plan or supervise its writing by someone you (or your client) hire.

Pick Venture Capitalists to Fund Your Deal

You know from earlier in this chapter what type of deal you have, either high tech or low tech. This is your first step in picking a venture capitalist. Your next step is to name the type of business you're in, such as

- Computers, electronics, artificial intelligence
- Entertainment, publishing, the arts
- Real estate, minerals, natural resources
- Consumer products, food, clothing
- Energy, oil and gas, solid fuels
- Transportation, airlines, shipping, trucking
- Any other specific business you can name

The above businesses, by the way, *are* actual types that venture capitalists think of when making investment decisions. You can't expect anyone to decide to put X million into a business that doesn't have some general name describing it!

You can get the names and types of projects favored by various venture capitalists from a directory of venture firms or from the "Venture Capital Millions Kit" described at the back of this book. The key in picking venture capitalists is to pick firms that favor your type of project (named like those above), who:

- Invest amounts in the range you need (don't expect the venture firm to exceed its limits).
- Put money into companies in geographic locations the venture firm prefers (many have *no* preference of any kind—they'll invest anywhere).

I suggest that you pick at least three venture capital firms. If you can find more, pick more. The more the better in this business!

Get Fast Answers With Your Executive Summary

Send one copy of your Executive Summary to each venture firm, using a letter like that in Figure 8.3. Wait for a response.

Your Letterhead (*printed*)
_____
_____

Tel. _____

XYZ Ventures Fund
123 Main Street
Anytown, U.S. 00000

Dear _____:

Enclosed is an Executive Summary for the ABC
Corporation that is seeking $1,000,000 in venture
capital for a most promising startup.

If this funding situation interests you, a complete
business plan is available from the undersigned. Please
call or write me, and I will send you the business plan
immediately.

We look forward to a favorable response.

Very truly yours,

Your Name and Title

Figure 8.3   *Typical Letter Submitting an Executive Summary to
a Venture Capitalist*

Venture capitalists *like* an Executive Summary inquiry because it saves them time. They can react in a few moments—either asking for a complete business plan or, unfortunately, declining interest. But my experience with hundreds of fundings shows that a venture capitalist will:

- React quickly to an Executive Summary inquiry.
- Be more likely to say "Yes" than when a full business plan is submitted "cold."
- Appreciate you trying to save their time by sending the Executive Summary first.
- May even call instead of writing to order the complete business plan, thereby saving more time.

If you want me to pick the venture capitalists for you, I will be glad to do so. Just write to me care of my newsletter at IWS, Inc., POB 186, Merrick, NY 11566–0186. You'll have to send me *nonconfidential* information in the form of an Executive Summary so that I can evaluate your proposal.

Those of you who use my "Venture Capital Millions Kit," mentioned earlier will have an Executive Summary prepared at *no* charge for as many deals as you find. These summaries are prepared quickly and returned to you. If, in my opinion, a deal is not fundable by venture capital, I will tell you!

We've now reached the point where you collect your fee for raising venture capital for a client, using one or more of the Executive Summaries you prepared (or had someone prepare) and the venture firms you picked. To ensure that your fee is paid, use a letter of agreement like that in Figure 8.4. You can change the suggested wording, if you wish. Just be sure to have an attorney approve your final version.

Become Your Own "Bank" With Venture Capital

If you want to make money on OPM, venture capital is one of the best ways I know. And forming your own venture capital fund, where you become the venture capitalist, puts you in the "banking" business—on OPM! You can get started without putting up one penny of your own.

Agreement to Pay Finders Fee

We, the undersigned, agree to pay _____Your Name_____
of _____Your City and State_____, a Finders Fee of $
_____ and _____% first year, _____%
second year, _____% third year, of our gross
profits derived from the finding supplied to us by
_____Your Name_____ .

Signed _____ Title _____

Company Name _____

Address _____

Phone _____ Date _____

Official To Receive Information

Name _____ Title _____

Date _____ Signature _____

Promptly upon receipt of this signed form, I will
forward to you all information I have on this finding.

Sincerely,

Your Name

Figure 8.4 *Typical Finder Agreement for Finding Venture Capital*

What is a venture capital fund? It's an organization that you can start yourself as a limited partnership that raises money from people seeking to invest in new ventures. Each limited partner buys one or more units (or participations) for $5000 or more, thereby raising as much as $50 million to be used in deals *you* select as worthy investments. Thus, *you* are a true venture capitalist, giving you power in investment decisions of all kinds.

Dozens of new venture capital funds are formed, funded, and operated every year. Yours could be the next one. You could soon own your own "bank" with millions of dollars of OPM available for investments you choose. To form a venture capital fund limited partnership:

1. *Prepare* a prospectus (a business plan) describing the fund and its investment objectives (to make the limited partners' money grow over the years).
2. *Tell* who will manage the fund, in addition to you. It's always good to have an attorney and an accountant on your management team to control investments. They'll be paid out of the interest earnings of the fund at the start and out of profits later on.
3. *Be specific* about the types of investments you'll make. Name businesses such as computers, electronics, real estate, and entertainment. Don't be so general that people want to turn away from your fund because they can't figure out what you're trying to do! Being specific lets (and helps) people decide what would be a wise decision for them with respect to your fund.
4. *Decide* if you'll sell your fund to the general public to raise really big bucks ($25 million and up) or sell it privately to raise up to $25 million. The choice is yours. If you go public, you'll have to register your offer with the SEC. Although this may sound frightening, it really isn't. All you need is a good attorney who knows the regulations and can guide you in what to do. As a general tip, go public if you don't have access to a number of investors (such as large companies or pension funds). Go private if you can tap into investors willing to put in at least $5000 a unit.
5. *Get the money* you seek. Immediately put it into a safe,

interest-earning investment such as Certificates of Deposit or U.S. Government Bonds. Keep some money on hand for operating funds—your salary, the salaries of others helping you, rent for an office, telephone charges, and the like.

6. *Start looking* for investments to make. You can do this by taking out classified ads in business newspapers and magazines, talking to local business people, and attending venture capital club meetings.

7. *Make* your first investments in firms you and your advisors (accountant and attorney, for example) believe can promise big profits for your fund. Watch each firm carefully to see that it grows the way you want it to so as to deliver the expected profits.

8. *Build your fund's* investments as time goes by. Be sure to pick profitable deals so your fund gets stronger with time.

Now how does your venture capital fund become your "bank"? It becomes your "bank" in a number of ways. It gives you big bundles of cash to control—just like being a bank. Then you and your advisors can distribute money to outside firms you believe in—just like a bank. Your reputation will improve enormously at every bank you deal with when you place fund money in the bank for temporary holding. True, a venture capital fund isn't a "bank" in the normal sense of that word. But to entrepreneurs looking for money, your venture capital fund is every bit a "bank," maybe even more so than the local institution on the corner of Main Street in your town!

So get into the best business ever invented—the money business in which *you* make money on OPM. It's easy to get started, the business is fun, and it can make *you* rich. Make venture capital funds *your* way to great wealth, starting right now!

Form a Venture Capital Club to Grow Your Wealth

Venture capital clubs are the latest rage around the world. Why? People have discovered that a free, capitalistic economy frees up people's energies so they produce more, thus providing a larger income and greater material wealth to everyone involved. This leads to a stronger nation and greater independence for its citizens.

Truly, good friend, the world has discovered what *you* already know, namely that:

- Having your own business gives you ultimate freedom while allowing people to express themselves in many different ways and encouraging original thinking that leads to a better life for all.

Remember, good friend, that it was in the United States that the transitor—the forerunner of all modern solid-state electronics—was invented. And it was in a garage in California where the personal computer was invented. And I could go on—with dozens of other inventions—to show that small businesses release a positive force into the world.

Venture capital clubs help this positive force grow by providing places where:

- Start-up and mature businesses meet venture capitalists seeking new deals.
- Venture capitalists meet people seeking money for business deals.

Here's how venture capital clubs work in most areas of the world today:

1. Monthly meetings are held in a local hotel or motel dining room at either breakfast or lunch (usually lunch).
2. Attendees pay for their own meals—typically $20 or $25, depending on the area.
3. Entrepreneurs sit at tables with venture capitalists, allowing for an exchange of ideas.
4. Each entrepreneur seeking capital is allowed either one or two minutes to describe his or her need to the assembled venture capitalists over the public address system. If deals are to be worked out, they're discussed after the presentations.

What's in it for you, if you form a venture capital club in your area? Plenty. Just look at these benefits:

- You get to know plenty of local venture capitalists because they'll be glad to attend your meetings.
- You get to know plenty of local entrepreneurs—people looking to get money for their firms.
- You can earn fees finding money for entrepreneurs; with so many deals available, you can pick the best for yourself.
- You become known as the local "deal host"—the person who brings money and the need for money together. This is an excellent reputation to have—people will "beat a path to your door," opening up many new opportunities for *you*.

Is it hard to form a venture capital club? No, it isn't. The simple steps you can take are as follows:

1. *Pick a name* for your club. Most clubs take either their state or city name. Thus, you might have the "Three Rivers Venture Capital Club" for your name if you're in the Three Rivers area.
2. *Announce the formation* of your club. Do this by sending out typed news releases like that shown in Figure 8.5. You can change the wording to suit your club. Send this news release to local newspapers, magazines, clubs, Chamber of Commerce, Rotary Club, Business Development Agency, and the like. These organizations will "spread the word" further about your club.
3. *Arrange for meetings with a local hotel.* Do this after you set your schedule of breakfast or luncheon meetings for the next six months. It's a good idea to include the dates for your first six meetings in your news release, as shown in Figure 8.5. Also include the price of the meeting. The hotel will give you the price per head (which means per person). Add a suitable amount to this to cover your costs, at least $10 a person.
4. *Plan your meeting format.* The usual meeting has a guest speaker who speaks free of charge because the publicity is good for him or her. The speaker comes on after diners have finished the main course and talks for fifteen to twenty minutes. There can be a question-and-answer period after the talk, if the speaker wishes. Then come the one- to two-minute

---

News Release—For Immediate Release

_____Your Name_____, president of the Three Rivers Venture Capital Club, announced formation of the club at a meeting today at the River House Inn. The objectives of the club, according to ___Your Name___ _____, are to bring local and national entrepreneurs together with venture capitalists to encourage funding of new and existing firms. To help in this work, entrepreneurs are urged to make a two-minute presentation about their companies to the venture capitalists in the audience.

Monthly meetings will be held on the third Tuesday of each month in the River House Inn. These luncheon meetings will feature a fifteen-minute talk by an experienced businessperson, followed by a question-and-answer period. Cost of attending the luncheon is $50 for nonmembers of the Three Rivers Venture Capital Club, $25 for members. Annual membership fee of the club is $150. All businesspeople are eligible to join.

Further information about the club can be obtained from _____Your Name_____ at _____ _____. The club's telephone number is _____.

Figure 8.5 *Example of a Venture Capital Club Announcement*

presentations from attendees. Arrange to have microphones in the center of the room so that the attendees can get to them quickly and make their presentations. After the meeting, the attendees can meet with venture capitalists in the same room where the meeting was held.

You won't get rich from the proceeds of your venture capital club. But being president of your own club will get you fame in your local area. Deals *will* start coming your way. You may even start doing Executive Summary work, as mentioned earlier. This will bring in quick cash to you.

So look around you today. A venture capital club may be just what the "doctor ordered" for your area. If you use my "Venture Capital Millions Kit," we'll be glad to send you our venture capital club list and data as a bonus. See the back of this book for details.

Making Money From Executive Summaries

As you know by now, the Executive Summary is today's entry to a venture capitalist's wallet. You can make money preparing Executive Summaries for firms seeking venture capital. Here's what you do:

1. *Run a classified ad* in your local business paper (or large-city newspaper) saying:

   NEED VENTURE CAPITAL? We help you get it. Call 123–4567 day or night.

   or

   VENTURE CAPITAL HELP. We show you how, where. Call 123–4567 day or night.

2. *When you get calls* (or you can have the readers of your ad write you) tell the respondents that you can prepare Executive Summaries, which may get them venture capital for their businesses sooner. Your fee will be $250 for each Executive Summary prepared, including selecting suitable venture capitalists to whom you'll send the approved Summary.

3. *Be flexible in your fee.* If the firm doesn't have much money, you can reduce the fee to, say, $125. But I recommend that you start with the $250 fee because this will earn you more money.

4. *Get information on the company,* described earlier. You can get this by mail or in person, depending on how you want to work. Do *not* accept confidential information. It can only lead to trouble if it leaks out. You'll be blamed even though you kept all the information locked up from the moment you got it.

5. *Write the Executive Summary.* You have two guides in Figures 8.1 and 8.2. Users of my "Venture Capital Millions Kit" get free preparation of Executive Summaries by me. My summaries will probably be no better than yours. But they *are* prepared by a pro who has done it before!

6. *Use a written agreement* (Figure 8.4) to cover your fee. Do *not* deliver the Executive Summary until *after* the written agreement covering your fee is signed by your client.

7. *Deliver the Executive Summary* by mail and collect your fee. We normally deliver three copies of the summary. If you're asked to prepare or to supervise the preparation of a business plan, follow the tips given earlier in this chapter.

Yes, venture capital *can* be *your* way to wealth on OPM. It's a great field that's exciting, rewarding, and fulfilling. Now's the time for *you* to consider getting into this great field! And I'm here to help you.

CHAPTER 9

RAKE IN GOLD FROM THE SALT OF THE EARTH

IF YOU MAKE IT BIG on Other People's Money with creative financing today, you'll almost certainly be involved in the "salt of the earth" — *real estate.* Why?

Real estate *is* an OPM business. And real estate *uses* creative financing more than any other business in the world. Note that I said *business.* Real estate *is* a business. Once people forget that, they're liable to wind up broke as some well-known real estate "experts" recently have.

Decide if Real Estate Is for You

You can make money from real estate in many ways. The most common way — and the one that people think of when real estate is mentioned — is ownership of buildings that give you monthly income. But there are other ways to make big bucks from real estate on OPM. Here are a number of ways, including the first:

- Ownership of income property like apartment houses, factories, shopping centers, and warehouses
- Leasing space that you sublet to others, making a profit on the difference between what you charge and what you pay
- Getting options to buy or rent property for a fully refundable small sum and selling or leasing at a profit to others before the option expires

- Getting raw land or other property on a contract basis and selling or improving using OPM
- Taking over repossessed property for zero-cash down and renting or selling to others
- Investing your real estate profits in tax-free municipal bonds used to build and operate real estate projects of various types
- Any other way you can figure out to make money from land, buildings, or the paper associated with them

To help you decide if real estate *is* for you, I'll point out several features of this *business* you should keep in mind. These features are as follows:

- Real estate is a *borrowed-money business*—people rarely put up much of their own money.
- Real estate is a relatively *safe business*—well-located property of any kind almost always goes up in value as time passes.
- Real estate is a *people business* to some extent—you *do* have to deal with real estate brokers, attorneys, sellers, and buyers.
- Real estate is a *slower business* than many other types of activities—your money may come in more slowly and sales take longer. Yet the value is there, day and night.
- Time works *for you* in real estate—the longer you hold property, the higher it goes in value and the larger the profit you make on the sale.
- You can get started in real estate with just $1 in your hand, and you can go on to wealth from this small start—all on OPM with creative financing.

You *can* get rich in some aspect of real estate on borrowed money. How can I say this? I can say it because I have thousands of letters from readers telling me how they're going from flat broke to great wealth using creative financing. Here's one such letter:

After reading *How to Borrow Your Way to Real Estate Riches* by Ty Hicks, we thought we'd give it a try. So we inquired at a local bank if they would give us a loan on a $6000 rental property. One week later they loaned us $7000. Tomorrow we're buying our second property with no money down, plus repair money. Not bad after having a bankruptcy three years ago. Your wealth-building ideas really work.

So take *your* pick of real estate as your business, if you wish. I'll assume that you decide that real estate *is* for you. Now, let's get started!

Try Property Ownership for Your Millions

With property ownership you acquire buildings, land, and even yacht docks that give you a regular monthly income. Thus, as one reader writes, "After reading one of your books I went out and bought my first four-plex. It has made me money every day since."

Most BWBs going into real estate start with an apartment house or other multifamily building. Some even start with single-family homes. Let's look at the advantages and disadvantages of each:

APARTMENT HOUSES	SINGLE-FAMILY HOMES
Seldom 100 percent vacant; almost always have a monthly income	Can be 100 percent occupied or 100 percent vacant; can have zero monthly income
Show a positive cash flow (money to you) most of the time	Can give modest income per house; many houses needed for big bucks
Can be financed easily if in good condition	Can be obtained for zero-cash (or near-zero) down
Big units require a professional manager	Can be managed by a beginner using his or her head

You *can* get apartment houses and single-family houses for zero-cash down! How can this be done? Take these easy steps, now:

1. Get a copy of your local, Sunday large-city newspaper.
2. Open to the real estate section; turn to the "Buildings for Sale" or "Apartment Houses for Sale" column.
3. Read *every* ad in the column; note facts like these: asking price, cash down required, price per unit (apartment), income, expenses, and property location.

4. Cut out the ads that interest you; mount them in a notebook you got for just this purpose.

5. Visit the properties that interest you; ask the seller for income and expense statements (you will be supplied these *free*).

6. Look over the property with your own eyes; see it as a *business.* Ask yourself: Will this property make money for me?

7. Go back home and compare the properties you've seen, along with their income and expense statements. Which looks best? Rate each property on a scale of one to ten, with the highest score going to the *best* property.

8. Continue looking for at least four weeks — six weeks would be better. Make notes on the condition and appearance of every property you see. Decide which would be best for you to own, from an income standpoint.

9. Talk to the seller; see if you can get the cash down payment requested reduced. The less cash you put down, the easier it will be for you to borrow the money, like the writer of the first letter above. Ask the seller if he or she will take back a second mortgage in place of cash. Work hard at getting this zero-cash benefit for yourself. Pay the asking price if zero-cash down can be arranged. Otherwise, if you can't arrange zero-cash down, then wheel and deal to reduce the asking price by 10 to 15 percent — there is almost always that much "pack" added to the asking price, in anticipation that the buyer will seek a lower price.

Keep looking until you find the property that you can get for zero-cash down. It *can* be done. This reader who writes did:

> I purchased several homes over the last several years. But Friday I closed a twelve-unit apartment complex for no-money down, a $225,000 value for $185,000. I assumed first and second mortgages, and the owner gave a third with interest only. Ty, I know I'm on my way now, and I just wanted to thank you for the knowledge.

This BWB did everything I recommend to *you.* Namely,

he worked out a zero-cash down deal by assuming two existing
mortgages and taking a new one for the cash-down payment
and he negotiated a reduction in the asking price, from
$225,000 to $185,000—a 17.8 percent decrease in the asking price. So you see, it *can* be done today, almost everywhere!
And I want *you* to be the next reader who writes me a winning
letter like that above.

Single-Family Homes Can Make You Rich

Some BWBs feel safer with single-family homes. Why?
There are a number of sensible reasons. Namely, single-family homes, in general, are easier to manage than apartment
houses; single-family homes are easier to buy than larger
apartment houses; and single-family homes are easier to find
and buy with zero-cash down. All these reasons are valid and
true. But there are two truths about single-family homes that
you must keep in mind at *all* times, namely:

- You *must* be able to rent a single-family home for more
  than its total operating cost—namely, *all* mortgage
  payments, real estate taxes, and a modest amount for
  maintenance and insurance.
- You *must* be able to keep every single-family home you
  own (except the one you live in) fully rented *all* the
  time. If you don't, the house will be a drain on your
  finances.

There are ways around the single-family home problem.
These ways can be used *after* you find suitable single-family
homes in your area. (I do *not* recommend buying outside your
own area until after you've had some actual experience with
this type of rental property.) To find single-family homes in
your area, follow the same nine steps given above for apartment houses. But, in addition, take these two easy steps:

- Check the rent levels for single-family homes in your
  area by looking in the same Sunday paper at listings under "Homes for Rent." Check to see if the rent will
  cover the necessary payments listed above—mort-

gages, real estate taxes, insurance, and maintenance. You *must* have a positive cash flow (money in fist every month) from *every* single-family home you own.

- Check with banks for their REO properties (Real Estate Owned) and with the tax assessor's office to see if they have any zero-cash down properties. They will often have bargains for you.

Don't limit yourself to single-family stand-alone homes. You can also make money renting condos and co-ops located in multiunit buildings like this reader who writes:

> Recently I bought Ty Hicks' *How to Make One Million Dollars in Real Estate in Three Years Starting with No Cash.* I personally began buying real estate a year ago when I was twenty-one and had no credit. Since that time I bought a beautiful home, two co-op apartments, a five-family and a six-family, all for no down payment. They appraise for just under $800,000. It still amazes me, a year later, that I am able to own real estate.

The best way to make money from single-family homes of any kind is to own a whole string of them, say twenty or thirty. Then you have what I call a "horizontal apartment house." If one or two units are vacant, you'll still have a large enough cash flow so you don't have to use personal funds to make payments on any of your homes. Here's a reader who's doing just that. He writes:

> In the past year I have been able to acquire six properties—five single-family houses and one four-unit building—from lists of HUD (Housing and Urban Development Administration) and VA (Veteran's Administration) foreclosures and have taken over each property with at least a 25-percent discount. In two cases, the VA sold to me at over 30-percent discount and provided 100-percent fixed-rate financing for thirty years. By best estimate, these properties are valued at $435,000 with combined equities of $126,000. Though this effort has required some work, I'm amazed at how easy it has been. About a year and a half ago I began reading books in preparation for retirement, including those by yourself. I'm really pleased with the results.

Make Money Without Owning Property

But suppose property ownership "turns you off." What then? You might want to try making money from real estate without owning one square inch of property! How can that be done? Here's one way:

- *Look around* your area to see what kind of rental space is in short supply (that is, there are more people looking for desirable space than there is available).
- *Decide which type of space* would be the best money maker for you—residential, office, commercial, or factory, for example. This plan usually works best with business space of some kind.
- *Check typical rents* per square foot for the type of space that interests you. You can get this information from local papers, local real estate brokers, and owners of buildings for rent.
- *See if you can get a reduction* in space-rent costs if you rent large amounts at one time. You can often save 10 to 25 percent of the square-foot cost if you rent large blocks of space at one time.
- *Make a quick survey* to see what rent you might charge, net, net, net for the space you're thinking of renting. (Net, net, net means your tenant pays the maintenance, taxes, insurance, and/or other payments.)
- *Decide* if you can make money on the difference between what you pay to rent the space and what you can get in rent. For example, you can rent space at $9 a square foot per year in blocks of 10,000 square feet. In smaller blocks, say 1500 square feet, you can charge and get $12 a square foot per year, net, net, net. Thus, you'll earn $3 a year per square foot rented. With 100,000 square feet to rent, your annual gross income would be $3 a square foot per year × 100,000 square feet = $300,000. But you'll have to subtract some expenses like advertising, telephone, and travel. If these total $40,000 a year, you'll still take home $300,000 − $40,000 = $260,000 a year. Not bad for someone who doesn't own a square inch of property!

You will, of course, have to work at finding suitable property to rent. This takes looking, walking (shoe leather), nego-

tiating, and thinking. But your take-home pay can really be
worth all your effort. Especially when you don't have any pes-
ky bosses looking over your shoulder, telling you what they
want done — yesterday!

Use Options to Make a Real Estate Fortune

Another way to make money from real estate without
owning any property is to use options to buy or lease. With an
option you're able to control a property for thirty, sixty, ninety
days or longer, depending on the terms of your option. During this time the property owner: must continue to do all
maintenance of the property, must continue to pay real estate
and other property-related taxes, and may not sell or lease —
depending on the option — the property to someone else
without paying *you*.

To take an option on a property, you do *not* need a real
estate broker's or salesperson's license. You do *not* need a license of any kind. You're as free as a bird — you can do what-
ever you want (within the law) to earn a profit on the option
you took. And, in many deals, you can get your option "ear-
nest money" deposit back if the deal does not go through. To
enjoy this benefit, your option *must* be written by a competent
attorney who knows real estate.

How do you get sellers or people wanting to lease property to search you out? That's simple. You just run a low-cost
classified ad in your local paper's real estate section that says

> HIGH PRICES PAID for superior real estate. Give us
> a ninety-day purchase option and see the results! Call
> 123-4567 now.

or

> SELL YOUR PRIME REAL ESTATE FASTER! Give
> us a ninety-day purchase option and watch the results.
> Call 123-4567.

When you get calls, pick the best offers and ask that you
be sent details of the property. You should get data on: asking

price, cash down payment, income, if any, and expenses. From these properties, pick the best ones for you based on your thoughts as to which type of property is easiest to sell or lease at this time. Once you know which properties are for you, offer an option to the seller or lessor for the longest period possible — usually ninety days.

- If this offer is accepted, have an attorney prepare the option wording. Do *not* try to write the final option yourself; you *do* need an attorney for this important document.
- Be sure to have a return clause in the option so that your money is returned to you if you can't sell the property or get the needed financing.

With your option properly signed, go back to your classified ads in your local and/or national papers, depending on where you think your greatest chance of selling is. Your ad can read:

SUPERIOR INCOME PROPERTY for sale. Great price, excellent income, long-term financing. Call 123-4567 day or night.

or

EXCELLENT INCOME PRODUCER for sale. Superior earnings can be yours. Full info available; call 123-4567.

Once you get some answers, send copies of the property information to the hottest prospects. You can have these sheets photocopied at low cost. Your price for the property should be at least 10 percent higher than the option price. For example:

Option price (your cost) is $350,000.

Your price to buyer is $385,000. Thus, you have $35,000 "to play with" — that is, to pay for your ads, closing costs, attorney, and other expenses. You should net at least $25,000 on this deal if you have the typical costs. Not bad for a ninety-day or less deal!

Note that with options you deal with the *best* real estate. You don't have to fool with fixer-uppers, rehabs, or distressed properties. Not that these are bad—you *can* make money from them—but it takes a special kind of person to get rich on these types. More about this later.

A lease option is like a buy option, except that it only covers the renting of a property or a certain amount of space, say 100,000 square feet for ten years. You handle leasing the same way—with classified ads—as selling. Your profit comes from the *difference* between what you pay to lease and what you charge for rent on the space.

Options allow you to control real estate *without* owning it. And, you *can* make money from options on almost *no* investment of any kind. But if even the small fee for an option is a major hurdle for you, read on to see how and where to get OPM for real estate wealth building.

How and Where to Get Real Estate Money

In real estate there are two basic types of loans. These loans can be described as:

- Short-term loans (up to five years) for smaller amounts of money—up to 25 percent of the cost of the property you're buying.
- Long-term loans (up to forty years) for larger amounts of money—up to 80 percent (sometimes 90 percent) of the cost of the property.

Long-term loans are usually easy to get. Why? They are made with the property as the collateral—that is, they are long-term mortgages. Because real estate *is* a borrowed-money business, everyone:

- Understands long-term mortgages (from fifteen to forty years on good property).
- Expects a long-term mortgage to be put on any property that's bought or sold because few people have enough money to pay all cash for a property.
- Is "in sync" for a long-term mortgage—that is, they did it for their home, their father did it, and so on. So they *expect* and want to make a long-term mortgage loan on every property that's bought and sold.

Because of these traditions and beliefs, it's easy to get the 75 percent long-term mortgage on a property. Lenders willthrow money in your face for a mortgage on a good property.And, sometimes, you can *assume* (take over) the existing mortgage on a property, thus avoiding closing costs, loan origination fees, and the like associated with the long-term mortgage.

Where BWBs run into problems is with the short-term loans for the property down payment, closing costs, and the rest. I recommend that you try to get a zero-cash down on *every* real estate deal. But if you're not able to, then you'll have to come up with some cash—namely borrowed money—also called OPM. Recognize here and now that:

- If you buy real estate with all borrowed money, you have a zero-cash deal because you do not have any of your own money in the transaction.

Also, nearly every zero-cash deal involves at least *two* loans—the large long-term mortgage loan—termed a *conventional mortgage*—plus a down-payment loan of some kind. Or, you may need a small loan to pay the closing costs. Where can this loan money come from? It can come from

- A personal signature loan you obtain.
- A loan on one or more of your credit cards.
- A second or third mortgage given to you by the seller of the property (purchase-money mortgage).
- A long-term loan that covers the down payment because the property is selling at far below its appraised value.

To show you what I mean by the zero-cash deal that you get without putting up any of your own money, here are two letters from readers:

In three days we are closing on an eleven-unit apartment building. We obtained a first mortgage,* and the balance we secured with a purchase-money mortgage. So there is no cash.

and

---

*This is the long-term mortgage mentioned above.

Within the last year I bought two eight-unit apartment buildings at a time when I had no money. I used 100 percent borrowed money. Both apartment buildings are in my own home town, population 1300. As a result of these two real estate purchases, I have within the year increased my net worth from $8000 to $50,000 after improvements and rent increases.

And when it comes to using your line of credit on your credit card(s), see if you can duplicate what this reader writes in a recent letter:

We're especially interested in obtaining more credit cards for down-payment dollars. So far we've bought eight converted apartment houses in this small college town (including one three-bedroom single-family) with credit card dollars—zero dollars out of pocket. A total of twenty units with a positive cash flow of over $800 per month. So our credit card payments are made by renters! That's over $300,000 worth of property—and all within one year. I have quit my job of truck driving to manage, maintain, and improve our houses.

To show you more clearly what I mean by zero-cash purchases of real estate, see Figure 9.1. In it we use a property having a total cost of $100,000. This, of course, is a lower-priced property in today's market. But the ideas at work for this property are valid for a $500,000 property, a $1 million property, and higher. You just multiply the numbers by the correct factor—5 for $500,000, 10 for $1 million, and so on.

As you can see in Figure 9.1, your down payment can be made up of any number of money sources—a credit-card loan, personal signature loan, or a purchase-money mortgage from the seller. The main point to remember here is:

- Zero-cash buys of property rarely come from just a long-term mortgage. You must almost always have more than one loan to get zero-cash real estate. Very few long-term mortgage lenders will lend you 100 percent of the money you need. They all want you to have some cash in the deal, but most don't care where you get the money. These lenders just want you to have some cash in the deal.

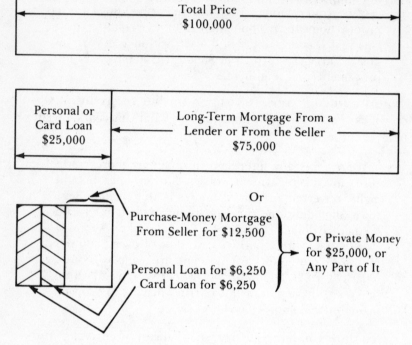

Figure 9.1. *How Zero-Cash Purchase of Real Estate Works*

Note that you might get *private money*—a loan from a friend or another person making such loans—to cover your down payment. You still will have zero cash of your own money in the deal.

There are times when a property will sell at far below its appraised value. Say the $100,000 property above is appraised at $100,000 market value, but the seller is willing to sell it for $60,000 because he wants a very fast deal.

You might be able to get the $75,000 long-term conventional mortgage based on 75 percent of the appraised value. If you did, you'd then have $15,000 ($75,000 − $60,000) for closing costs and other expenses. If these ran $5000, you'd *mortgage out* with $15,000 − $5000 = $10,000 cash MIF (Money In Fist), tax-free!

Although mortgaging out—also called 110 percent, 120 percent, and so forth financing—*is* possible, it does take more work than just getting loans for the cash down payment. But it can and does happen with great frequency. All you have to do is find the deal that can support this kind of financing. Every day you find such deals by *looking* for them.

Your long-term mortgage is easy money. Why? There are thousands of lenders in this business. Such lenders include:

- Banks, insurance companies,
- Credit unions, mortgage companies,
- Savings and loan associations, the federal government,
- Many others.

Remember, your credit rating has little to do with getting a long-term mortgage. Why? The property is the main collateral for the loan. Thus, you may be able to get a long-term mortgage loan on good property even though your credit history isn't the best. So—as I often tell readers—a good property can become your "financial umbrella" sheltering you from the rains of earlier money problems.

If you want lists of names, addresses, and telephone numbers of long-term mortgage lenders, you should have a copy of *2500 Active Real Estate Lenders.* See the back of this book for details about it.

If you ever have a real estate deal you need financed and you can't find a suitable lender, I suggest you check copies of my newsletter *International Wealth Success.* And if you're a subscriber, I'll be glad to research for you, free of charge, lenders who might finance *your* deal. And when I say free of charge I mean *no* points, *no* fees, and *no* retainers to me!

Go With the Flow in Today's Real Estate

Real estate is a great *business*—remember that word *business!* Some of the most creative financing ideas in the world have been "wrapped around" real estate. That is, real estate encourages all kinds of creative financing. And this creative financing can make *you* rich if you have the courage and drive to put it to use.

And, as in any other business, real estate has "fashions" that come and go. If you go with these "fashions" you can make quick money on OPM and build real estate wealth. Here are some current ways *you* can go with the flow in today's world of creative real estate thinking and finance:

- Buy condos and rent them out; get rich on the rise in value.
- Buy "occupied apartments" and hold until the renters move out.
- Buy and rent out dock condos, called dockominiums

Let's take a fast look at these three ways of going with the flow. Of course, there are plenty of others. But these three will help you recognize and evaluate other creative trends.

Get Rich on Condos

Today many people shy away from grass cutting, home maintenance, and the other chores associated with home ownership. Yet these same people want a place of their own. How do they combine both wants? They buy, if they can afford it, a condo apartment. But what about people who want a condo apartment but can't afford it? What do they do? They *rent* a condo apartment!

You can make money by buying condo apartments — often with zero-cash down — and renting them out. How can I say this? I've loaned money to a number of people who're doing just this. And I have the ultimate proof because:

- Every person who borrowed money from me has repaid his or her loan *in full.*
- Every loan has been paid off in full *ahead of time* because the BWB real estate investors made money on the condo rent — they had a *positive cash flow.*
- They all sold their condos at a very good profit, making money on the deal.

How can you get in on condo riches? It's easy. Just take these simple steps, starting right now, if condos interest you:

1. Get your reliable large-city, Sunday newspaper and turn to the "Real Estate" section.
2. Look for condo apartments for sale in your area.
3. Start your notebook as detailed earlier, making notes of prices, square footage, location, and the like.
4. Concentrate on studio and one-bedroom condos at the start. Why? These are most attractive to young professionals and singles — your primary market for renters.
5. Go out and visit some of the condos that appeal to you. See each apartment as a renter would — its location, view, and size.
6. Compare your monthly *carrying charges* for the condo(s) you like with typical rentals charged in the area. To do this, look in the "Apartments for Rent" column and make notes of the rent for a studio, a one-bedroom, and so on in the area of your condo.
7. You *must* have a *positive cash flow* each month. This means the rent you receive *must* be more than your carrying charges. For example, with carrying charges of $650 a month and a rental income of $725 a month, your positive cash flow will be $725 − $650 = $75 per month. You must *not* accept a rent less that $650 a month.
8. Get the cash down payment for your condo (this is usually only 10 percent of the total price) from a personal loan, credit card loan, or private money. In many condos your monthly rental income will be enough, after paying your carrying charges, to pay for your down-payment loan also. So you own the condo free and clear — another example of OPM creative financing on zero cash.

Hold your condo for as long as you want while you watch it go *up* in value! The price of your condo will rise at least 5 percent a year. Thus, the second year you own a $100,000 condo, it will sell for at least $105,000. Many condos rise 10 percent a year and some 15 percent. In those conditions your $100,000 condo will be worth $110,000 and $115,000, respectively, in the second year.

"Spin the Wheel" on Occupied Apartments

In many large inner cities there are *occupied apartments* for sale. These apartments are in buildings that have gone condo or co-op, and the tenant of the apartment chose *not* to buy the unit. However, the owner of the building wants to sell the apartment. So the apartment is offered for sale at anywhere from 10 to 30 percent of its market value—based on the tenant being allowed to stay in the apartment as long as he or she wishes—provided his rent payments are made on time. Here's what you get:

- Title to a good apartment that you own
- Rental income every month from your tenant
- A chance "to make a killing" on the sale of the apartment when the tenant moves
- Responsibility to pay the monthly maintenance on the apartment—this is usually less than the monthly rent you get so you're in a positive cash-flow situation

When the tenant moves or has to be moved out because he or she dies, you have the full right to occupy the apartment yourself, if you wish, rent the apartment to someone else, or sell the apartment at a profit. A typical investor in occupied apartments opts to sell the unit as soon as it becomes vacant. This way they show an immediate profit on the sale. Why? Well, they paid only 10 to 30 percent of the market value of the apartment. Because the unit will sell at market value or just slightly less, you get an instant profit. Let's look at a recent sale:

```
Market value of the apartment  = $100,000
Price investor paid, occupied   =   30,000
Sales price                     =   99,000
Profit before costs             =   69,000
Closing costs                   =    2,000
Rental profit at $50 per month
  for 12 months                 =      600
Net profit on investment        = $67,600
```

The above investor held the apartment twelve months before the tenant moved out. During this time the investor earned a profit of $50 a month on the rent from the unit, above the maintenance costs.

If occupied apartments interest you as a real estate investment, look into the opportunities in a large city near you. When you pick an apartment, keep these facts in mind:

- The older the tenant, the sooner—usually—you'll have the apartment ready for sale.
- Buy the most desirable apartment, even if the tenant is younger—you'll make more on its sale.
- Accept only those apartments giving you a positive cash flow.
- Be ready for the long haul—your tenant may live to 100 years or more!

Get a String of Condos for Your Future Wealth

In many areas of the country you can buy well-built condos in highly desirable areas (on a golf course, on a lakefront, or overlooking a beautiful valley, for example) for very modest prices and just small down payments. You then rent out each condo to give you a positive cash flow. Here's a real-life example:

Condo price	=	$85,000
Monthly cost of mortgage, maintenance, other charges	=	800
Typical rent in area per month	=	900
Positive cash flow	=	100

What do *you* get out of such a deal? You get a positive cash flow of about $100 a month—typically $1000 a year, on average—plus the chance to share in the rise in value of the condo. Often, your tenant, after living in the unit a few years, will want to buy it. This is good because you will not have to pay the usual 6 percent real estate broker's fee on the sale.

One word of caution: If the condo string appeals to you, buy *only* condos. Do *not* buy co-op apartments. Why?

- With co-ops, tenants must be approved by the co-op

board, leading to long delays and loss of money for you.
• Boards often limit renting to just one year, no more.

With a condo, you can rent the unit to anyone *you* choose. There is *no* need to get approval from anyone but yourself. So simplify your rental life—invest only in condos. You'll be glad you did!

Look Into Miniwarehouses in Your Area

If you'd like a real estate business that takes almost no supervision, then a miniwarehouse or ministorage building might be for you. These buildings rent out space to people who want to store excess items such as books, clothing, files, pictures, and furniture. Some operators will rent you a four-feet by four-feet space eight feet high. But most rent eight by eight, ten by ten, and so on. Some rents are as high as $20 a year per square foot. So a ten by ten space brings in $2000 a year.

Your costs in operating a ministorage building are very low. You just have your:

• Mortgage payment
• Real estate taxes
• A little heat and a little light
• Some labor, usually at the minimum hourly wage.

Some miniwarehouse operators use their ministorage buildings as a "cash cow" while waiting for the land in the area to rise in value. This way they make a profit in two ways:

• From the nice miniwarehouse income.
• From the rise in the value of the land when they sell.

Just recognize that miniwarehouses combine both an operating business and the real estate that can rise in value. You're providing space for nonliving items, instead of living beings as in apartment houses.

Go Boating While Profiting From Real Estate

Land in desirable areas, even when that land is under water, rises in value every second of the day. For example, take land in boating areas around the world. Developers are selling condo docks where:

- You buy a dock for a boat of a certain length—typically thirty to seventy feet.
- You get the dock and the right to the land between it and the next dock for a number of years, often ninety-nine years.
- You do, however, have to pay certain monthly charges associated with the dock; these, however, are small.
- You can use your dock for *your* boat or rent the dock to another boat owner at anywhere from $50 to $150 per foot of *dock* for six months.
- Watch the dock condo go up in value every second of the day and night! For example, a forty-two-foot boat dock in my area recently sold for $63,000 just two years after it sold for $31,000! The owner more than doubled his money in two years. And the whole deal was financed on borrowed money—OPM!

Get Foreign Money for Your Deals

As you know by now, I'm a strong believer in borrowed money used in a creative manner. And foreign money—also called offshore money—can be your answer to OPM if:

- You have access to new, well-located downtown properties.
- You have access to new office structures that are being built or were recently finished.
- You have access to new or recently opened shopping centers.

Get the point at the start: Overseas money *likes* new or relatively new real estate in good areas of town. You can't (usually) get funds from overseas for rundown property in poor areas. But there *is* plenty of money out there for good properties. And overseas money:

- Will often accept a lower return than domestic money, looking for eventual increases in returns.
- Can supply almost unlimited funds quickly without lots of red tape if the investors like the property you have.

Foreign money can be yours after you get some real estate experience. For the BWB it's best to look for local money at the start. Once you have a few nice buildings, you can start looking for overseas funds. But don't overlook this enormous source of money.

Get on the Real Estate Wealth Trip

More of my readers have built wealth from real estate than from any other type of business. They write me almost every day saying something like what this reader writes:

> We, my wife and I, have been using the zero-cash concept for several years to acquire income property in our area. We currently own seventy-two units and are constantly looking for more. The current gross rental income is in excess of $100,000 per year. I am forty years of age. We have plans drawn for building a fifty-six unit apartment–townhouse project.

Another reader writes a happy letter, saying:

> I have used your methods since I started reading your wonderful *International Wealth Success* newsletter. I have used your methods, and I now have four apartment buildings worth about $450,000. Three years ago I had only a triplex but by using your methods of borrowing to the hilt, I have been able to acquire these four larger buildings.

There are hundreds of other ways to get rich in real estate. Only a few are covered in this book because we don't have enough space. If you want to learn other methods to get rich in real estate, I suggest that you read one or more of my other books, listed at the back of this one.

And remember this, good friend, I'm as close to you as your phone! If you have a tough real estate question, try me. I may have the answer, quickly and easily, for you. So start getting rich *now*, using OPM and creative financing to go from flat broke to great wealth. Then you may write, as this lady did:

> You are the gentleman who started us on the road to property ownership fourteen years ago. My husband and I now have about 235 units, of which about 150 are single-family dwellings. Thank you very much!

CHAPTER 10

LAUGH ALL THE WAY TO THE BANK: WILD, WORKABLE IDEAS FOR RAISING MONEY TODAY

As YOU'VE PROBABLY figured by now, I'm a "can do" type of person. And I want *you* to be the same when it comes to making money on OPM. Why? You *can* make money on OPM today more easily than ever before. I see it happen every day.

People sometimes come to me saying, "I tried twenty banks and couldn't get a loan." I ask, "Did you try a finance company?" The answer is, "Yes, and they said 'No,' also. It's impossible for me to get a loan." Their attitude is: Agree with me so I can tell the world I can't get a loan. These people seem to take satisfaction in their failures.

Yet I won't accept failure for you, for me, for anyone! Why? I see so much success against almost impossible money odds. As an example, this letter comes from a prisoner who has *no* job, *no* credit rating, *no* credit history:

>   I bought and read four of your books since being incarcerated (put in prison) two years ago. They've opened my mind to a brand new world. Through the guidance of your books, I started credit accounts at three banks and have obtained several credit cards. I have a credit ceiling of about $10,000. And I've done all this while a prisoner in the State of _____. The books of yours I've read are *How to Borrow Your Way to a Great Fortune, Smart Money Shortcuts to Becoming Rich, How to Start Your Own*

Business on a Shoestring and Make Up to $500,000 a Year, and *How to Build a Second Income Fortune in Your Spare Time.*

I'm being released in eighteen days, and I'm going straight. No doubt about it. Thanks to your books I no longer have to break the law to obtain a decent lifestyle.

If a prisoner can make it while behind bars, I'm sure you can make it while having all the advantages of complete freedom. Let's see how you can laugh all the way to the bank, using wild but workable ideas to raise money! Let me warn you that some of these ideas are way out. But they *do* and can work for you, if you work them.

Raise Money for Money

Get closer to money, and it will get closer to you! This is true for anyone who wants to make more money. How can *you* get closer to money? Get into the money business. How? Here are the easy steps:

1. *Decide* if you'd like to raise money for money. You'd work for charities, religious organizations, educational institutions, and the like.
2. *Pick* the type of organization with whom you'd like to work on a freelance basis. It's best at the start to specialize in one or two types of organizations—charities, schools, or churches, for example.
3. *Contact* several firms already doing fund raising for the types of organizations with whom you want to work. Ask for their free information. You'll find such firms listed under "Fund Raising" in your local "Yellow Pages."
4. *Study* the information you get. You'll see that most fund-raising firms work on a percentage of the money raised—typically 5 percent, but it may be higher or lower depending on the amount of work to do and the help available.
5. *Approach* by phone or mail local "targets" for whom you might raise money. Offer your services on a free basis with your pay coming from a percentage of the money you raise.

6. *Get* the organization to help you by supplying volunteer workers, plus names of people who might give to the fund drive.
7. *Put* your "show on the road" to start collecting money for your client. Take your percentage out as you deliver funds to your client.

Fund raising is a great business—one that you can start for just a few dollars and then start making money for yourself in days. As you gain experience you can branch out to other fields, if you wish. You'll get much closer to money every day. And I guarantee you that some will rub off on you!

How can I say this? I've run any number of fund-raising campaigns and watched as people got rich. I want *you* to become one of those people who get rich from money that you raise for others. Everyone's happy—your client, you, and your family. Not to mention me—the one who gave you the idea!

Take Over a Ghost Town and Make Money

There are hundreds of ghost towns around the world—places abandoned by former residents and allowed to decay. Yet such towns are often loaded with history. And they're a constant tourist attraction. Take over such a town, and you have many rights such as

- *Getting loans* from your state without personal credit checks or qualifying—the town is your credit "umbrella" for all deals.
- *Raising money* by the sale of municipal bonds to restore the town—its streets, buildings, sewers, and lights.
- *Earning money* from guided tours of the town and sale of historical photos and books.
- *Paying yourself* a salary as mayor, town supervisor, or some other official of the ghost town.
- *Setting up a fund* on a nonprofit basis to raise money from contributions to restore the town.

As you can see, you *will* get money from these and other sources when you take over a ghost town. And let me tell you that when you walk into a local bank in a nearby "live" town and tell the loan office "I'm Mayor _____ of Gold Rush Heights," you'll be given a great welcome. You might even walk out with a loan, a credit card, and an invitation to "See us, Mayor, if you ever need any other help in the future!"

Run a Credit Card Merchant Account

You can act as a merchant account for small stores, flea markets, garage sales, moving sales, and the like and earn big bucks while raising instant cash for yourself. What sort of a deal is this? You, with the approval of the credit card companies:

1. *Offer to process* credit card charges for firms that do not have their own merchant accounts.
2. *Are paid* a percentage of each charge you put through your merchant account.
3. *Get anywhere* from 5 percent to 25 percent of the charge with a cost to you of less than 2 percent!
4. *Have the money* credited to your bank account at the speed of light (186,000 miles a second) when you use a phone terminal to send your charges to your bank.
5. *Earn even more* if you use a low-cost toll-free 800 number for your customers who can call you and give you their charges on the phone. This way you can serve mail-order customers all over the country. You gain intelligence (what's selling for them, how many, and at what price) while earning money for yourself! And all of this can be done from your home with just one phone and one low-cost terminal.

This is a great business because you deal with just a few scraps of paper plus a telephone line. When you take orders through your 800 number, you charge your customers for this service also—often at $1 to $5 a call, depending on the amount of the order. Once you get the order, you put it through your merchant account and send a check to your client after approval of the charge by the credit card bank.

As throughout this book, you're working with OPM—

Other People's Money—and getting paid for it! If you're interested in getting step-by-step directions on making money from credit cards, get a copy of my "Cash Credit Riches Kit," described at the back of this book.

Other ways you can make money from credit cards include:

- Helping people get secured credit cards.
- Helping people get loans on their credit card lines of credit.

Let's take a look at how you can get money for yourself from these two businesses.

Make Money From Credit Cards

You can make money helping people get credit cards. Then you'll laugh all the way to the bank because you're making money from the bank's services. In helping people get credit cards, the best approach is:

- Guide people to getting *secured* credit cards.
- Where a small deposit—$300 to $500—secures the credit that the bank extends to the person.
- Allow them to buy items or services costing up to one-half or three-quarters (depending on the bank) of the amount deposited.
- You earn a fee of anywhere from $50 to $250 for each secured card you get for a person.
- Your fee depends on how much work you do and how bad the person's credit rating is, and some of them have very bad ratings at the start!

Not all banks issue secured credit cards. So you have to work with those banks that do issue such cards. A list of these banks (and there are plenty of them) is contained in the "Cash Credit Riches Kit" mentioned above. It is not possible to give the list here because bank requirements are almost constantly changing, and the list would soon be outdated.

You can also make money helping people use the line of credit they have on their credit cards. Some cards go up to

$35,000, with plans to go to $50,000. This means that a person can write checks for up to $35,000:

- To be charged to his or her credit card account,
- With years to pay off the amounts charged to the card account.
- This money can be used for any legal purpose the cardholder chooses.

Why would someone look to you to use the line of credit? Many people are unsure about how to use their lines of credit, don't know what to use the money for to make it grow, and need sound business advice before they take their first step. As a financial consultant you can provide this advice for a fee. And, you can guide these clients into sound investments that will make their money grow while repaying the credit card loans. The usual fee for such work is $250 to $500, depending on the amount of work you'll do.

Use the Single-Payment Policy Approach

As a BWB your biggest problem in getting financing is the lack of suitable collateral for the lender to make you a loan. Most lenders seek some kind of "liquid" collateral to back up a loan, except for unsecured signature loans.

You may be able to rent stocks and bonds as collateral for a loan. To do this, you go to a stockbroker and ask if any of his or her wealthy clients would allow you to borrow their securities for use as loan collateral. You pay a fee—usually 5 percent of the loan amount—to the owner of the securities when you receive the loan. Although this method is popular, it has been pushed aside by the single-payment policy approach. In this method of getting collateral:

- You take out a single-payment life insurance policy from any of the major insurance companies.
- You use the loan proceeds to buy the policy at a cost of 30 to 60 percent of the amount the policy will pay at the end of its term or in the event of your demise before that.

- This gives your lender the assurance that the amount loaned *will* be repaid at the end of the policy life, which will coincide with the end of the loan time.
- You keep for business use the difference between the loan amount you receive and the cost of the single-payment policy. As noted above, the policy cost can run between 30 and 60 percent of the amount of the loan.

Putting this into an example, let's say that you seek a $100,000 loan. Your policy will cost, we'll say, 33 percent of the amount of the coverage. So you will have to take these steps to get your loan:

```
Amount of money needed for
  business                            =    $100,000
Cost of single-payment policy  =  33⅓ percent
Amount you must borrow          =    $303,000
```

The interest on the loan and the principal will be repaid by the amount paid for the policy in one payment, or $303,000 − $100,000 = $203,000. If you repay the loan on a monthly basis, then the $303,000 that the policy pays at the end becomes yours!

The only problem with the single-payment policy method is to find a lender who will accept a policy as collateral. At present, there are a number of lenders who like this type of collateral. So you should deal with such lenders when seeking a loan that has a single-payment policy as its collateral. Contact any large insurance company for data on these policies.

And while you're talking to an insurance agent, see if he or she has any interest in business or real estate investing. If the agent does, tell him or her that future commissions on policies already sold make excellent loan collateral. Most lenders will loan up to 75 percent of the value of these commissions.

Try Bank Funds to Get Bank Funds

Banks issue two types of "instruments" (pieces of paper) that can help *you* get money from the bank. Because these instruments are backed by the bank's money (funds), you—in effect—are using bank funds to get bank funds (money). The two instruments are:

- Banker's acceptance.
- A letter of credit.

Both are used in import-export and similar businesses. Here's how you might use each in your business—to laugh all the way to the bank.

A *banker's acceptance* is a piece of paper that a bank sells to its customers to get back money it loaned to a businessperson, often an importer. Say you want to import 1000 television sets costing you $150 each. You go to your favorite *commercial bank* and:

- Tell the banker that you need a loan of $150,000 ($150 per set − 1000 sets) to import 1000 television sets for which you already have a domestic buyer.
- The sets will be the banker's collateral for the $150,000 loan.
- A banker's acceptance can be used to get the money back quickly into the banker's hands so it can be loaned out to someone else.
- The bank's income comes from the difference between interest it charges *you* and the rate it must pay the buyer of the banker's acceptance.
- With most such acceptances running 90 to 180 days or even less in some cases.

So all you need to do to get funding through a banker's acceptance is to find a suitable product to import and get a buyer for it. This is much easier to do than it sounds if you deal with wanted products.

A *letter of credit* (L/C) is a simple letter from a bank stating that you can write checks against the bank up to a certain limit—say, $150,000, as above. The letter will state certain terms that govern your drafts (checks), such as the interest rate and amounts "taken down" (checks written) on each draft.

Most letters of credit are for import-export activities. But you can also use an L/C as collateral for a loan from another lender. Lender policies, however, vary on L/Cs used as collat-

lender. Lender policies, however, vary on L/Cs used as collateral. So before spending a lot of time and energy trying to get
and use an L/C as collateral, check with your potential lenders first. It can save you a lot of anguish.

Remember, L/Cs are issued by *commercial* (business)
banks. So don't try to get an L/C from an S&L—it won't
work. And while you're talking to your commercial bank, ask
if you can use back-to-back L/Cs. You can use these when you
are not the supplier or maker of goods you're exporting and
when you want to keep the name of the importer (your customer) and price being paid to you a secret.

With a back-to-back L/C, one L/C—in effect—guarantees another. The result is that you have a solid-gold transaction based on OPM without putting up one cent of your own.
Talk to your commercial bank; one conversation could make
you millions just like this reader who writes:

> Just returned from a three-month tour of the Middle
> East and Central America. Have executed three multi-
> million dollar contracts. Thank you, Ty. Had it not been
> for *International Wealth Success,* this would not have
> come to pass. I used contacts from *Worldwide Riches Op-
> portunities,* Volumes 1 and 2.*

"Frame" Your Money Request So You Get a Positive Reply

All lenders and money suppliers have favorite reasons for
lending money. If you can "tap into" these reasons and frame
your need in terms of one or more of them, "you've got it
made." Why? When your money need is in line with the supplier's business strategies:

* Your request seems "like a natural"—the lender or
  supplier feels at home with you.
* Loan officers or others in control of funds don't have
  to scratch their heads over approval. ("Because we've

*See the back of this book for details.

advanced funds for these reasons before, it's easy to do another one," says one officer.)

For example, one worldwide lending organization that works in million dollar-deals says in its ads:

Financing provided for leveraged buyouts, bridge loans, mezzanines, recapitalizations, restructurings, re-financings, term loans, turnarounds.

If you have a money need for any one or more of the above uses, I suggest that you contact such a lender. Your need will be right in line with their current lending policies. So you're much more likely to get a "Yes" response to your request.

How can you find out what a money supplier favors as reasons for lending money? It's easy—just take these steps:

1. *Define* the supplier. Is it a lender, a venture capital firm, or a grantor?
2. *Specify* what kind of funding *you* need—a loan, venture capital, or a grant.
3. *List* suppliers of your type of need.
4. *Contact* each supplier and get more details on his or her money supply policies—types of situations preferred, time limits if any, and collateral requirements.
5. *Tailor* your request to fit as many of these policies as you can.
6. Submit your application in neatly *typed* form—don't cut corners with handwritten applications.

Getting money is serious business. You can't approach it as a lark. Why? The suppliers will turn away from you. You must negotiate from a position of serious intent to earn money on other people's money so that they, as money suppliers, profit while you profit! One reader writes:

Thank you, Mr. Hicks. (*I'd really prefer if he called me Ty, as everyone does!*) Incidentally, I negotiated a $100,000 venture capital loan through the *International Wealth Success* newsletter ad I ran (free of charge as a subscriber). Thank you! May next year be your biggest money year ever!

Get Sure-Fire Cosigners to Help You

Many people tell me, "I don't have anyone to cosign for me" when I suggest they get a cosigner for a loan they need.* Yet I regularly get money for people who've been bankrupt, slow payers on loans, out of work and in debt, and turned down by dozens of lenders. How can you do the same—get a big loan with a not-so-good credit history? That's easy—get sure-fire cosigners. Who are they?

- Equipment suppliers. Have the supplier of equipment you need for a business cosign on the loan to buy the equipment.
- Real estate sellers. Have the seller of real estate cosign on the down payment loan you need to buy the property. Or, have the seller take out a home-equity loan for the down payment; you assume the home-equity payments.
- Franchisors. Have a franchisor cosign for you when you buy a franchise for a business. Can you think of any business stronger than a hamburger company, a muffler firm, an oil company? Your lender will jump with joy when you offer such collateral.

And, of course, the *real key* to using sure-fire cosigners has never been revealed in print before. That key?

Get your cosigner to cosign for more money than needed for the specific transaction. Thus, if you need a $100,000 down-payment loan, get your cosigner to cosign for a $150,000 loan. You'll get an extra, nontaxable $50,000 that you can use for operating capital! And, good friend, you'll *always* need a few extra dollars for such costs whenever you go into your own business on OPM.

Seek and Use Private Money Suppliers

Public money suppliers such as banks, finance companies, and large venture capital firms can be great sources of funds

*Be sure to try the "Global Cosigners and Money Finders Association"; see back of book.

for you. They can supply you with billions of dollars (OPM) to help you go from flat broke to great wealth with creative financing. But sometimes it's easier to get OPM from private lenders. Who are these money suppliers?

- Individuals with excess funds who want to earn more than a bank or a Certificate of Deposit can offer
- Groups of individuals who've pooled their funds to earn a greater return through a business investment
- Other types of investors—for example, companies and associations—seeking higher return or an "in" to another business

Private investors are easy to find. Where? The newsletter *International Wealth Success,* the *Wall Street Journal,* the *New York Times,* and the *Los Angeles Times* are examples. Just look in the "Money Available" columns. Using private investors will:

- Get you your money faster.
- Usually cost you a little more (sorry!).
- Seldom involve credit checks.
- Be strictly for business or income real estate money-making purposes.

With a private investor you won't have the fancy trappings of a bank. Instead, you may meet on a street corner and negotiate a loan under a streetlight. But the money will be just as useful and powerful. After all, it's OPM! Try some and see for yourself.

Tap Billion-Dollar Insurance Companies

If you're looking for *big* real estate money—$1 million and up—you should tap some of the billion-dollar insurance companies. They, in general, love strong real estate deals, and they have money coming out of their ears!

Insurance companies are picky about their deals. For example, they:

- Don't like small deals—many have a $1-million minimum, others a $5-million minimum.

- Prefer new properties that are clean, fresh, and well-built.
- May want an equity kicker—a small percentage of the ownership or a small percentage of the profit realized on the sale of the property.
- May want a takeout—that is, they want to finance your long-term mortgage after construction of a new project is finished. This is great in my view because it means that you don't have to run around looking for a long-term loan when the building is finished.

So keep insurance companies in mind! They're great to deal with and their treasury capacity will blow your mind.

Let Your Lender Sell You the Deal

People call me and ask my advice on financing. Some, though, can't stop talking long enough to get an answer. They just keep running off at the mouth. The result? They don't get any advice because they can't keep quiet long enough for it to be given!

These people often treat lenders the same way. The result? They don't get the loans they seek. To get the loan *you* need, take these easy steps—they will really line your pockets with OPM:

1. Let the lender suggest the amount of money you should borrow. Why? It makes the lender feel safer with the loan when you accept the amount the lender feels is "right" for your deal.
2. Let the loan officer be your adviser. Almost every loan officer is a frustrated wealth builder. He or she is afraid to go out and challenge the world. So each huddles and cringes in the "security" of a good job. (Few realize they can be laid off in an instant.) By allowing the loan officer to advise you, you are permitting him or her to live a dream and feel independent instead of being chained to a desk as a wage slave.
3. Be polite at *all* times. And keep your mouth shut! You hurt your loan chances almost every time you volunteer *any* information. Instead, answer all questions you're asked. Do this in a firm, sure voice but don't

brag. Don't make the loan officer feel deprived or in-
secure. There's no good reason for you to increase
anyone's insecurity.

Having a lender friend is probably the best kind of friend you
can have when building your wealth. So take time and energy
to cultivate as many lender friends as you can!

Accept a Standing Loan, if Offered

A *standing loan,* also called an *interest-only loan,* is one on
which you pay only interest each month, as compared to paying principal and interest (called P&I) each month. Let's take
a look at how the monthly payments compare.

You, we'll say, borrow $100,000 at 12 percent simple in-
terest for seven years. If you're paying P&I, your monthly
payment will be $1765.28. But with a standing loan, your
monthly payment will be only $1000 a month. So your pay-
ment is reduced by $765.28 a month. This means you'll have
more money for yourself or for the business.

Of course, at the end of the seven years you'll have to repay the full $100,000. But by this time your business will
probably be so strong that you will easily repay the full
amount. And during the seven years you'll be able to deduct,
fully, your monthly interest cost because it's a business
expense!

Get Tax-Haven Loans

There are many areas around the world that are tax ha-
vens—places where people and companies "park" money to
reduce, completely legally, their income taxes. Banks bulge
with money in such areas, so loans are often easier to get. But
you must know how to apply for such loans.

Rules vary from one locality to another, but you should
know that getting such loans may require that

- You have a local company in the tax-haven country; the
  cost of forming one is very low.

- You have a local attorney to represent you. This is easy because there are many attorneys set up to do this work at a small charge to you.
- You may have to transfer funds through a bank account in the tax-haven country to an account in your local bank. Again, this is easy.

Tax-haven loans should be at least $100,000. Why? The paperwork for a loan of this size is about the same as for a $10,000 loan. So most lenders prefer the larger loans.

Look to Your Credit Union

The credit union movement is one of the fastest growing money sources in the world today. How do I know? For some years I've been president and chairman of the board of a multimillion dollar credit union. I built it from assets of just $800,000 to assets of some $100 million! So I speak from intimate know-how!

Credit unions, although growing, have seen some of their loans almost dry up. A number of reasons account for this; it's the result that's important. Credit unions have moved to business loans to keep their loan portfolios at levels where they earn enough interest to pay dividends to members. You can take advantage of this situation. How?

1. Find out which credit unions in your area might allow you to join.
2. Do this by looking in your "Yellow Pages" under "Credit Unions" and calling or writing each.
3. Once you find some credit unions you can join, ask if they're making business loans.
4. If any credit unions are making business loans, join them. It's free and only requires that you fill out a simple membership card.
5. Once you've joined, look for the business or real estate deal that you like.
6. Apply for a business or real estate loan. Be sure to *type* your loan application. Ask for a loan for the amount

and purpose for which your credit union is lending. Then you'll have a good chance of getting the loan you seek!

Credit unions are great organizations. Used correctly, credit union money can make you rich. Look around today for your credit union opportunity to get OPM quickly, easily, and in a friendly atmosphere!

Get Surety-Bond Backing

A surety bond is like an insurance policy that guarantees that you will repay the loan. Surety bonds are issued by insurance companies and surety firms. For a modest premium, the surety bond:

- Guarantees loan repayment in the event you fail to repay.
- Assures the lender that the principal (the amount you borrow) is safe.
- Makes it much easier for you to get your loan quickly and easily.

To find out who issues surety bonds in your area, contact an insurance broker. They can quickly check local and national insurance companies and give you the prices charged. The surety bond must be in force *before* you get your loan money. Before paying for a surety bond:

- Check with the lenders you plan to use to see if a surety bond is acceptable.
- Find out if the bond issuer you plan to use is acceptable to the lender.
- Don't make a final choice of a surety bond until you have full answers from one or more lenders.

Surety bonds have been used for years to guarantee loans. Get a surety bond for the loan you need and you, too, can laugh all the way to the bank with your pockets bulging with OPM!

Use a Home-Equity Loan

The "rage loan" today is the home-equity loan. It's really a second mortgage on your home. People, however, are turned off by second mortgages. So lenders devised the home-equity handle—it sounds higher level and appeals to everyone.

Most home equity lenders will lend you 75 percent of the equity (value of the home, less what you owe on it). This can bring in big bucks—up to $1 million with some lenders.

And with a home-equity loan, the interest you pay *is* deductible on your tax return. This means that you get a tax break with such loans. To take advantages of this tax break and the millions available, see my newsletter *Money Watch Bulletin* described at the back of this book. It gives you monthly updates on the newest in home-equity loans, plus many other types of loans.

If you don't own your own home, perhaps you can bring in a partner who owns a home and can get a home-equity loan on it. The main key to keep in mind with money for business is:

Get your business funds in *any* honest way you can. If it means "hocking the kitchen sink," go ahead and get the money. Remember that money invested to make money in a sound business will almost always come back to you—many times over!

Get Money From Thirty-Eight Different Sources

Sometimes, when I'm driving to my yacht, sitting on an airplane, or awake early in the morning, I think of ways my readers can get money for their business or real estate ideas. Recently, on a Concorde flight to Europe, I jotted down this list of thirty-eight money sources for *you*. After each name there appears a letter. The letter *B* means that *business* funds can be obtained from the source; *R* means *real estate* funds can

be obtained from the lender. Here's your list of thirty-eight
sources of quick OPM for you:

1. Commercial banks   B, R
2. Savings and loan associations or banks   B, R
3. Mutual savings banks or associations   B, R
4. Mortgage companies or lenders   R
5. Insurance companies   B, R
6. Real estate investment trust   B, R
7. Commercial finance companies   B, R
8. Private lenders   B, R
9. Small Business Administration   B
10. Small-business investment companies   B, R
11. Venture capital firms   B,R
12. Farm Home Administration   R
13. Federal Housing Administration   R
14. Local bond issues for your firm   B,R
15. Industrial development agencies   B, R
16. Leasing finance firms   B
17. Large industrial firms   B, R
18. Housing and Urban Development
    Administration   R
19. State housing development agencies   R
20. State industrial development agencies   B, R
21. State job development agencies   B, R
22. Financial consultants   B, R
23. Stock underwriters   B, R
24. City and state real estate loans   R
25. Mortgage brokers and bankers   R
26. Securities firms; stock brokers   B, R
27. Insurance company "basket money"   R
28. Pension funds of all types   R
29. Trust companies   B, R
30. Credit unions (state and federally chartered)   B, R
31. Title companies   R
32. Veteran's Administration   B, R
33. Commercial paper   B
34. Banker's acceptance   B
35. Estate trustees   B, R
36. Compensating-balance loans   B, R
37. Loan societies   B, R
38. Overseas loan sources of all types   B, R

Use a Negotiable Promissory Note

You can speed sales and the flow of money into your bank account by using a *negotiable promissory note*. This is a promissory note you can take to any bank and turn it into instant cash. And such a note can be used for any of a variety of deals. Let's take a look at one. You, we'll say:

- *Have a service* you can sell easily to people if they don't have to invest much cash. This could be an option on a piece of real estate or an exercise gym contract.
- *Decide to take* a very small down payment with the balance on a promissory note. For example, if your service costs $5000, you decide to accept $250 down (5 percent) and a negotiable promissory note for $4500.
- *Get $500 immediately* and monthly payments on the promissory note. Should you decide you need instant cash, you can take the note to a bank and have it *discounted* (sold) for 80 or 85 percent of the current value of the note. Thus, if you took the note to a bank when its current value was $4000, you'd get $3200 (80 percent), or $3400 (85 percent) cash. The negotiable promissory note allows you to sell it whenever you want, without getting permission from the person who gave you the note.

Get an Open-End Mortgage

An *open-end mortgage* is a loan for more than the amount of money you need. Thus, let's say you need $200,000 for a real estate deal. You're able to get approval of a $250,000 loan, based on the appraised value of the real estate. Thus, you have $250,000 − $200,000 = $50,000 more than you need. You can take this extra $50,000 and:

- Put it into a safe, interest-bearing bank account, waiting for a good investment opportunity.
- Invest the money in another business, different from the real estate.

- Use the money to fix up the real estate, to allow you to raise rents and have a property worth more money.

An open-end mortgage often depends on getting a property for less than its appraised value. You can do this by looking for properties for sale at bargain prices!

Put Paper Collateral to Work

You can get OPM in big chunks and laugh all the way to the bank by putting paper collateral—pieces of paper—to work for you. You use paper collateral instead of real assets like land, buildings, inventory, or machinery. Why? Paper collateral is usually cheaper, faster, and less of a hassle than any other type. So consider these sixteen types of paper collateral, some of which are discussed elsewhere in this book:

1. Have a seller cosign on your loan.
2. Find a cosigner yourself—for a fee, possibly.
3. Use borrowed municipal bonds as collateral.
4. Use borrowed corporate bonds as collateral.
5. Have a bank savings account assigned as collateral.
6. Use a contract from a stable organization (the government or large corporation, for example) as collateral.
7. Assign promissory notes as collateral.
8. Get a government guarantee for your loan.
9. Use a purchase order issued to you as collateral.
10. Use warehouse receipts as collateral.
11. Use accounts receivable as collateral.
12. Use real estate or other leases as collateral.
13. Use two-name paper (in effect, a cosigner).
14. Work a zero-cash takeover with a line of credit.
15. Lease items that generate money; put no cash down.
16. Get loans for joint ventures with the other firm providing the collateral.

There are hundreds of other ways to get OPM to build your wealth to enable you to go from flat broke to great wealth. But we don't have space to cover all of them in this book. My newsletter *International Wealth Success* gives a number of these methods in its monthly issues. And my many other books, listed at the back of this book, give hundreds of additional ways to get OPM.

"Do these methods work?" you ask. I have thousands of letters from readers throughout the world telling me how these methods worked for them. These letters are open for inspection by you or anyone else. All I need is a day's notice that you want to inspect the actual, signed letters. I'll get them out of the safe, and you can enjoy reading them. You'll read letters saying:

> I subscribe to the *IWS* newsletter and bought two Ty Hicks courses and almost all of his books. Using the info from these publications, I recently obtained a loan to start a toy distributor business with no difficulty whatsoever.

and

> I would like to thank you for showing me how to do the following: (1) Buy improved lots at good prices on my terms with no-money down, after banks and private parties were not interested in helping me. I have forty lots in one section and twenty-two in another; I'm going to build modular housing on them. (2) Buy two separate radio stations worth over $1 million for only $2000 of my own money.

and

> After reading your books, I found myself getting up and going. I bought some apartments and townhouses with your no-money down ideas, which worked wonderfully. At present I'm working on a private hospital in Europe using your techniques.

and

> Through one tip from you during a telephone conversation, I was able to make contact with one source who has assisted us in placing in excess of $10 million this month. Of course, this is the culmination of several months of concentrated effort. Considering the complexity of the deals, they would have been virtually impossible without your help.

and

> I got a $6000 home improvement loan, a $10,000 second mortgage loan, and a $4000 loan to pay off our car. All my thanks go to you. Your newsletter is worth every cent.

and

> We're off and running. Borrowed $407,000 as follows: $100,000 equity loan, $231,000 land-acquisition loan, $76,000 signature loan, total $407,000. *You said it could be done!* Cost of property was $390,000. All money borrowed from savings and loan, which has our home mortgage. Same bank is giving us construction money, too. When we found the right bank, *they* sold *us* on our own project.

and

> In the past six months we bought four pieces of real estate totalling $2,650,000 for $4 down payment—$1 on each deal. And we have just gained control of another piece of property (via option with no expiry date) valued at $5,850,000—again with no money down.

I could go on and on. But I think you *do* get the point, namely you *can* get rich today in a business you like, using *borrowed money* to go from flat broke to riches while having lots of *fun* and *not being bothered* by surly, nasty, complaining bosses who threaten you. In this book I've tried to show *you* how to get rich today on OPM. My other books and newsletters will also help. And I'm ready to help—every day and night—if you want to write or call me. Try me and see!

BIBLIOGRAPHY

Other Profit-Building Tools from Tyler Hicks' *INTERNATIONAL WEALTH SUCCESS* Library

As the publisher of the famous *INTERNATIONAL WEALTH SUCCESS* newsletter, Ty Hicks has put together a remarkable library of dynamic books, each geared to help the opportunity-seeking individual — the kind of person who is ready and eager to achieve the financial freedom that comes from being a SUCCESSFUL entrepreneur. Financial experts agree that only those who own their own businesses or invest their money wisely can truly control their future wealth. And yet, far too many who start a business or an investment program of their own do not have the kind of information that can make the difference between success and failure.

Here, then, is a list of publications hand-picked by Ty Hicks, written especially to give you, the enterprising wealth builder, the critical edge that belongs solely to those who have the *inside* track. So take advantage of this unique opportunity to order this confidential information. (These books are *not* available in bookstores.) Choose the publications that can help you the most and send the coupon page with your remittance. Your order will be processed as quickly as possible to expedite your success. (Please note: If, when placing an order, you prefer not to cut out the coupon, simply photocopy the order page and send in the duplicate.)

IWS-1   **BUSINESS CAPITAL SOURCES.** Lists more than 1,500 lenders of various types — banks, insurance companies, commercial finance firms, factors, leasing firms, overseas lenders, venture-capital firms, mortgage companies, and others. $15. 150 pgs.

IWS-2   **SMALL BUSINESS INVESTMENT COMPANY DIRECTORY AND HANDBOOK.** Lists more than 400 small business investment companies that invest in small businesses to help them prosper. Also gives tips on financial management in business. $15. 135 pgs.

IWS-3   **WORLDWIDE RICHES OPPORTUNITIES,** Vol. 1. Lists more

194

than 2,500 overseas firms seeking products to import. Gives name of product(s) sought, or service(s) sought, and other important data needed by exporters and importers. $25. 283 pgs.

IWS-4   ***WORLDWIDE RICHES OPPORTUNITIES***, Vol. 2. Lists more than 2,500 overseas firms seeking products to import. (Does NOT duplicate Volume 1.) Lists loan sources for some exporters in England. $25. 223 pgs.

IWS-5   ***HOW TO PREPARE AND PROCESS EXPORT-IMPORT DOCUMENTS.*** Gives data and documents for exporters and importers, including licenses, declarations, free-trade zones abroad, bills of lading, custom duty rulings. $25. 170 pgs.

IWS-6   ***SUPPLEMENT TO HOW TO BORROW YOUR WAY TO REAL ESTATE RICHES.*** Using government sources compiled by Ty Hicks, lists numerous mortgage loans and guarantees, loan purposes, amounts, terms, financing charge, types of structures financed, loan-value ratio, special factors. $15. 87 pgs.

IWS-7   ***THE RADICAL NEW ROAD TO WEALTH*** by A. David Silver. Covers criteria for success, raising venture capital, steps in conceiving a new firm, the business plan, how much do you have to give up, economic justification. $15. 128 pgs.

IWS-8   ***60-DAY FULLY FINANCED FORTUNE*** is a short BUSINESS KIT covering what the business is, how it works, naming the business, interest amortization tables, state securities agencies, typical flyer used to advertise, typical applications. $29.50. 136 pgs.

IWS-9   ***CREDITS AND COLLECTION BUSINESS KIT*** is a 2-book kit covering fundamentals of credit, businesses using credits and collection methods, applications for credit, setting credit limit, Fair Credit Reporting Act, collection percentages, etc. Gives 10 small businesses in this field. $29.50. 147 pgs.

IWS-10   ***MIDEAST AND NORTH AFRICAN BANKS AND FINANCIAL INSTITUTIONS.*** Lists more than 350 such organizations. Gives name, address, telephone, and telex number for most. $15. 30 pgs.

IWS-11   ***EXPORT MAIL-ORDER.*** Covers deciding on products to export, finding suppliers, locating overseas firms seeking exports, form letters, listing of firms serving as export management companies, shipping orders, and more. $17.50. 50 pgs.

IWS-12   ***PRODUCT EXPORT RICHES OPPORTUNITIES.*** Lists over 1,500 firms offering products for export — includes agricultural, auto, aviation, electronic, computers, energy, food, healthcare, mining, printing, and robotics. $21.50. 219 pgs.

IWS-13   ***DIRECTORY OF HIGH-DISCOUNT MERCHANDISE SOURCES.*** Lists more than 1,000 sources of products with full name, address, and telephone number for items such as auto products, swings, stuffed toys, puzzles, oils and lubricants, CB radios, and belt buckles. $17.50. 97 pgs.

IWS-14   ***HOW TO FINANCE REAL ESTATE INVESTMENTS*** by Roger Johnson. Covers basics, the lending environment, value, maximum financing, rental unit groups, buying mobile-home parks, and conversions. $21.50. 265 pgs.

IWS-15   ***DIRECTORY OF FREIGHT FORWARDERS AND CUSTOM HOUSE BROKERS.*** Lists hundreds of these firms throughout the United States which help in the import/export business. $17.50. 106 pgs.

IWS-16   ***CAN YOU AFFORD NOT TO BE A MILLIONAIRE?*** by Marc Schlecter. Covers international trade, base of operations, stationery, worksheet, starting an overseas company, metric measures, profit structure. $10. 202 pgs.

IWS-17   ***HOW TO FIND HIDDEN WEALTH IN LOCAL REAL ESTATE*** by R. H. Jorgensen. Covers financial tips, self-education, how to analyze property for renovation, the successful renovator is a "cheapskate," property management, and getting the rents paid. $17.50. 133 pgs.

IWS-18   ***HOW TO CREATE YOUR OWN REAL-ESTATE FORTUNE*** by Jens Nielsen. Covers investment opportunities in real estate, leveraging, depreciation, remodeling your deal, buy- and lease-back, understanding your financing. $17.50. 117 pgs.

IWS-19   ***REAL-ESTATE SECOND MORTGAGES*** by Ty Hicks. Covers second mortgages, how a second mortgage finder works, naming the business, registering the firm, running ads, expanding the business, and limited partnerships. $17.50. 100 pgs.

IWS-20   ***GUIDE TO BUSINESS AND REAL ESTATE LOAN SOURCES.*** Lists hundreds of business and real-estate lenders, giving their lending data in very brief form. $25. 201 pgs.

IWS-21   ***DIRECTORY OF 2,500 ACTIVE REAL-ESTATE LENDERS.*** Lists 2,500 names and addresses of direct lenders or sources of information on possible lenders for real estate. $25. 197 pgs.

IWS-22   ***IDEAS FOR FINDING BUSINESS AND REAL ESTATE CAPITAL TODAY.*** Covers raising public money, real estate financing, borrowing methods, government loan sources, and venture money. $24.50. 62 pgs.

IWS-23   ***HOW TO BECOME WEALTHY PUBLISHING A NEWSLETTER*** by E. J. Mall. Covers who will want your newsletter, planning your newsletter, preparing the first issue, direct mail promotions, keeping the books, building your career. $17.50. 102 pgs.

IWS-24 **NATIONAL DIRECTORY OF MANUFACTURERS' REP-RESENTATIVES.** Lists 5,000 mfrs.' reps. from all over the United States, both in alphabetical form and state by state; gives markets classifications by SIC. $28.80. 782 pgs., hardcover.

IWS-25 **BUSINESS PLAN KIT.** Shows how to prepare a business plan to raise money for any business. Gives several examples of successful business plans. $29.50. 150 pgs.

IWS-26 **MONEY RAISER'S DIRECTORY OF BANK CREDIT CARD PROGRAMS.** Shows the requirements of each bank listed for obtaining a credit card from the bank. Nearly 1000 card programs at 500 of the largest U.S. banks are listed. Gives income requirements, job history, specifications, etc. $19.95. 150 pgs.

IWS-27 **GLOBAL COSIGNERS AND MONEY FINDERS ASSOCI-ATION.** Publicize your need for a cosigner to get a business or real estate loan. Your need is advertised widely under a Code Number so your identity is kept confidential. $50.

IWS-28 **WALL STREET SYNDICATORS.** Lists 250 active brokerage houses who might take your company public. Gives numerous examples of actual, recent, new stock offerings of start-up companies. $15. 36 pgs.

Success Kits

K-1 **FINANCIAL BROKER/FINDER/BUSINESS BROKER/CON-SULTANT SUCCESS KIT** shows YOU how to start your PRIVATE business as a Financial Broker/Finder/Business Broker/Consultant! As a Financial Broker YOU find money for firms seeking capital and YOU are paid a fee. As a Finder YOU are paid a fee for finding things (real estate, raw materials, money, etc.) for people and firms. As a Business Broker YOU help in the buying or selling of a business — again for a fee. See how to collect BIG fees. Kit includes typical agreements YOU can use, plus 4 colorful membership cards (each 8 × 10 in.). Only $99.50. 12 Speed-Read books, 485 pgs., 8½ × 11 in., 4 membership cards.

K-2 ***STARTING MILLIONAIRE SUCCESS KIT*** shows YOU how
to get started in a number of businesses which might make
YOU a millionaire sooner than YOU think! Businesses covered
in this big kit include Mail Order, Real Estate, Export/Import,
Limited Partnerships, etc. This big kit includes 4 colorful membership cards (each 8 × 10 in.). These are NOT the same ones
as in the Financial Broker kit. So ORDER your STARTING
MILLIONAIRE KIT now—only $99.50. 12 Speed-Read
books, 361 pgs., 8½ × 11 in., 4 membership cards.

K-3 ***FRANCHISE RICHES SUCCESS KIT*** is the only one of its kind
in the world (we believe). What this big kit does is show YOU
how to collect BIG franchise fees for YOUR business ideas
which can help others make money! So instead of paying to use
ideas, people PAY YOU to use YOUR ideas! Franchising is one
of the biggest businesses in the world today. Why don't YOU
get in on the BILLIONS of dollars being grossed in this business today? Send $99.50 for your FRANCHISE KIT now. 7
Speed-Read books, 876 pgs., 6 × 9 & 8½ × 11 in. & 5 × 8 in.

K-4 ***MAIL ORDER RICHES SUCCESS KIT*** shows YOU how YOU
can make a million in mail order/direct mail, using the known
and proven methods of the experts. This is a kit which is different (we think) from any other—and BETTER than any other!
It gives YOU the experience of known experts who've made
millions in their own mail order businesses, or who've shown
others how to do that. This big kit also includes the Ty Hicks
book "How I Grossed More Than One Million Dollars in Mail
Order/Direct Mail Starting with NO CASH and Less Know-
how." So send $99.50 TODAY for your MAIL ORDER SUC-
CESS KIT. 9 Speed-Read books, 927 pgs., 6 × 9 & 8½ × 11
in.

K-5 ***ZERO CASH SUCCESS TECHNIQUES KIT*** shows YOU how to
get started in YOUR own going business or real estate venture
with NO CASH! Sound impossible? It really IS possible—as
thousands of folks have shown. This big kit, which includes a
special book by Ty Hicks on "Zero Cash Takeovers of Business
and Real Estate," also includes a 58-minute cassette tape by Ty
on "Small Business Financing." On this tape, Ty talks to YOU!
See how YOU can get started in YOUR own business without
cash and with few credit checks. To get your ZERO CASH
SUCCESS KIT, send $99.50 NOW. 7 Speed-Read books, 876
pgs., 8½ × 11 in. for most, 58-minute cassette tape.

K-6 ***REAL ESTATE RICHES SUCCESS KIT*** shows YOU how to
make BIG money in real estate as an income property owner, a
mortgage broker, mortgage banker, real estate investment

trust operator, mortgage money broker, raw land speculator, and industrial property owner. This is a general kit, covering all these aspects of real estate, plus many, many more. Includes many financing sources for YOUR real estate fortune. But this big kit also covers how to buy real estate for the lowest price (down payments of NO CASH can sometimes be set up), and how to run YOUR real estate for biggest profits. Send $99.50 NOW for your REAL ESTATE SUCCESS KIT. 6 Speed-Read books, 466 pgs., 8½ × 11 in.

K-7 ***BUSINESS BORROWERS COMPLETE SUCCESS KIT*** shows YOU how and where to BORROW money for any business which interests YOU. See how to borrow money like the professionals do! Get YOUR loans faster, easier because YOU know YOUR way around the loan world! This big kit includes many practice forms so YOU can become an expert in preparing acceptable loan applications. Also includes hundreds of loan sources YOU might wish to check for YOUR loans. Send $99.50 NOW for your BUSINESS BORROWERS KIT. 7 Speed-Read books, 596 pgs., 8½ × 11 in.

K-8 ***RAISING MONEY FROM GRANTS AND OTHER SOURCES SUCCESS KIT*** shows YOU how to GET MONEY THAT DOES NOT HAVE TO BE REPAID if YOU do the task for which the money was advanced. This big kit shows YOU how and where to raise money for a skill YOU have which can help others live a better life. And, as an added feature, this big kit shows YOU how to make a fortune as a Fund Raiser—that great business in which YOU get paid for collecting money for others or for yourself! This kit shows YOU how you can collect money to fund deals YOU set up. To get your GRANTS KIT, send $99.50 NOW. 7 Speed-Read books, 496 pgs., 8½ × 11 in. for most.

K-9 ***FAST FINANCING OF YOUR REAL ESTATE FORTUNE SUCCESS KIT*** shows YOU how to raise money for real estate deals. YOU can move ahead faster if YOU can finance your real estate quickly and easily. This is NOT the same kit as the R.E. RICHES KIT listed above. Instead, the FAST FINANCING KIT concentrates on GETTING THE MONEY YOU NEED for YOUR real estate deals. This big kit gives YOU more than 2,500 sources of real estate money all over the U.S. It also shows YOU how to find deals which return BIG income to YOU but are easier to finance than YOU might think! To get started in FAST FINANCING, send $99.50 today. 7 Speed-Read books, 523 pgs., 8½ × 11 in. for most.

K-10   ***LOANS BY PHONE KIT*** shows YOU how and where to get
business, real estate, and personal loans by telephone. With just
32 words and 15 seconds of time YOU can determine if a lender is interested in the loan you seek for yourself or for someone
who is your client—if you're working as a loan broker or finder. This kit gives you hundreds of telephone lenders. About
half have 800 phone numbers, meaning that your call is free of
long-distance charges. Necessary agreement forms are also included. This blockbuster kit has more than 150 pages.
8½ × 11 in. Send $100 *now* and get started in one hour.

K-11   ***LOANS BY MAIL KIT*** shows YOU how and where to get business, real estate, and personal loans for yourself and others by
mail. Lists hundreds of lenders who loan by mail. No need to
appear in person—just fill out the loan application and send it
in by mail. Many of these lenders give unsecured signature
loans to qualified applicants. Use this kit to get a loan by mail
yourself. Or become a loan broker and use the kit to get started. Unsecured signature loans by mail can go as high as
$50,000 and this kit lists such lenders. The kit has more than
150 pages. 8½ × 11 in. Send $100 *now* to get started in just a
few minutes.

K-12   ***REAL-ESTATE LOAN GETTERS SERVICE KIT*** shows the
user how to get real estate loans for either a client or the user.
Lists hundreds of active real estate lenders seeking first and ju-
nior mortgage loans for a variety of property types. Loan
amounts range from a few thousand dollars to many millions,
depending on the property, its location, and value. Presents
typical application and agreement forms for use in securing
real estate loans. *No* license is required to obtain such loans for
oneself or others. Kit contains more than 150 pages. 8½ × 11
in. Send $100 *now* to get started.

K-13   ***CASH CREDIT RICHES SYSTEM KIT*** shows the user three
ways to make money from credit cards: (1) as a merchant account, (2) helping others get credit cards of their choice and (3)
getting loans through lines of credit offered credit card hold-
ers. Some people handling merchant account orders report an
income as high as $10,000 a day. While this kit does not, and
will not, guarantee such an income level, it *does* show the user
how to get started making money from credit cards easily and
quickly. The kit has more than 150 pages. 8½ × 11 in. Send
$100 *now* to get started soon.

K-14   ***PROFESSIONAL PRACTICE BUILDERS KIT*** shows YOU
how to make up to $1,000 a week part time, over $5,000 a week
full time, according to the author, Dr. Alan Weisman. What

YOU do is show professionals — such as doctors, dentists, architects, accountants, lawyers — how to bring more clients into the office and thereby increase their income. Step-by-step procedure gets you started. Provides forms, sample letters, brochures, and flyers YOU can use to get an income flowing into your bank in less than one week. The kit has more than 150 8½ × 11 in. pages. Send $100 *now!* Start within just a few hours in your local area.

K-15 ***VENTURE CAPITAL MILLIONS KIT.*** Shows how to raise venture capital for yourself or for others. Gives steps for preparing an Executive Summary, business plan, etc. You can use the kit to earn large fees raising money for new or established firms. $100. 200 pgs.

K-16 ***GUARANTEED LOAN MONEY.*** Shows how to get loans of all types—unsecured signature, business, real estate, etc.—when your credit is not the strongest. Gives full directions on getting cosigners, comakers, and guarantors. $100. 250 pgs.

Other Recommended Business Books

P-1 ***HOW TO START A BUSINESS ON A SHOESTRING AND MAKE UP TO $500,000 A YEAR*** by Tyler G. Hicks. Shows the beginning entrepreneur how to start a money-making business for as little as $100 and go on to make a fortune. Included is a comprehensive list of over 1,000 GREAT BUSINESSES YOU CAN RUN OUT OF YOUR OWN HOME. Special Value at only $9.95. 255 pgs.

P-2 ***TRAVEL FREE! HOW TO START AND SUCCEED IN YOUR OWN TRAVEL CONSULTANT BUSINESS*** by Ben and Nancy Dominitz. This is the only book that shows you the inside track to running your own profitable travel business from home. $19.95. 208 pgs., hardcover.

P-3 ***THE COMPLETE FRANCHISE BOOK: EVERYTHING YOU NEED TO KNOW ABOUT BUYING OR STARTING YOUR OWN FRANCHISE*** by Dennis L. Foster. Read this before investing a dime! This book will walk you step by step and in plain English through each phase of the franchise formula, from understanding the Uniform Franchise Code to negotiating the best deal. A must for anyone thinking about owning or starting a franchise. $17.95. 250 pgs., hardcover.

P-4   **SEVEN STRATEGIES FOR WEALTH AND HAPPINESS** by
&   Jim Rohn. America's foremost business philosopher tells YOU
P-5   why most people fail to succeed and HOW to make sure YOU
      break away from the pack. A must for anyone seriously inter-
      ested in having a fully successful life. Book (P-4) $13.95, 156
      pgs., hardcover. Six-cassette album (P-5) $65.

P-6   **WINNING THEM OVER** by Jim Robinson. Every business-
      person must promote his business to succeed. Yet most people
      fail to get their messages across effectively. Now you can learn
      how to give winning speeches that will make people admire
      YOU. In addition, you'll be shown, step by step, how to get lo-
      cal TV and newspaper attention for your product or business.
      $17.95. 285 pgs., hardcover.

P-7   **TV PR** by Wicke Chambers and Spring Asher. Learn how to
      get free TV publicity. Why pay thousands of $$$ when YOU
      can be the honored guest of talk show hosts and anchormen
      free of charge? This is the only book exclusively devoted to get-
      ting YOU in front of tens of thousands of people free of
      charge. $24.95. 121 pgs. plus photographs, deluxe cloth
      edition.

ORDER FORM

Dear Ty: Please rush me the following:

☐ IWS-1	Business Capital Sources	$15.00	_____
☐ IWS-2	Small Business Investment	15.00	_____
☐ IWS-3	World-wide Riches Vol. 1	25.00	_____
☐ IWS-4	World-wide Riches Vol. 2	25.00	_____
☐ IWS-5	How to Prepare Export-Import	25.00	_____
☐ IWS-6	Real Estate Riches Supplement	15.00	_____
☐ IWS-7	Radical New Road	15.00	_____
☐ IWS-8	60-Day Fully Financed	29.50	_____
☐ IWS-9	Credits and Collection	29.50	_____
☐ IWS-10	Mideast Banks	15.00	_____
☐ IWS-11	Export Mail-Order	17.50	_____
☐ IWS-12	Product Export Riches	21.50	_____
☐ IWS-13	Dir. of High-Discount	17.50	_____
☐ IWS-14	How to Finance Real Estate	21.50	_____
☐ IWS-15	Dir. of Freight Forwarders	17.50	_____
☐ IWS-16	Can You Afford Not to Be . . . ?	10.00	_____
☐ IWS-17	How to Find Hidden Wealth	17.50	_____
☐ IWS-18	How to Create Real Estate Fortune	17.50	_____
☐ IWS-19	Real Estate Second Mortgages	17.50	_____
☐ IWS-20	Guide to Business and Real Estate	25.00	_____
☐ IWS-21	Dir. of 2,500 Active Real Estate Lenders	25.00	_____
☐ IWS-22	Ideas for Finding Capital	24.50	_____
☐ IWS-23	How to Become Wealthy Pub.	17.50	_____
☐ IWS-24	National Dir. Manufacturers' Reps	28.80	_____
☐ IWS-25	Business Plan Kit	29.50	_____
☐ IWS-26	Money Raiser's Dir. of Bank Credit Card Programs	19.95	_____
☐ IWS-27	Global Cosigners and Money Finders Assoc.	50.00	_____
☐ IWS-28	Wall Street Syndicators	15.00	_____
☐ K-1	Financial Broker	99.50	_____
☐ K-2	Starting Millionaire	99.50	_____
☐ K-3	Franchise Riches	99.50	_____
☐ K-4	Mail Order Riches	99.50	_____
☐ K-5	Zero Cash Success	99.50	_____
☐ K-6	Real Estate Riches	99.50	_____
☐ K-7	Business Borrowers	99.50	_____
☐ K-8	Raising Money from Grants	99.50	_____
☐ K-9	Fast Financing of Real Estate	99.50	_____
☐ K-10	Loans by Phone Kit	100.00	_____
☐ K-11	Loans by Mail Kit	100.00	_____
☐ K-12	Real Estate Loan Getters Service Kit	100.00	_____
☐ K-13	Cash Credit Riches System Kit	100.00	_____
☐ K-14	Professional Practice Builders Kit	100.00	_____
☐ K-15	Venture Capital Millions Kit	100.00	_____
☐ K-16	Guaranteed Loan Money	100.00	_____
☐ P-1	Business on a Shoestring	9.95	_____
☐ P-2	Travel Free!	19.95	_____
☐ P-3	The Complete Franchise Book	17.95	_____
☐ P-4	Seven Strategies (book)	13.95	_____
☐ P-5	Seven Strategies (cassettes)	65.00	_____
☐ P-6	Winning Them Over	17.95	_____
☐ P-7	TV PR	24.95	_____

Total Amount of Order _____

Order form is continued on back of this page

I am paying by: ☐ Check   ☐ MO/Cashier's Check   ☐ Visa/MC

Name: _____

Address: _____

City: _____ State: _____ Zip: _____

Visa/MC#: _____ Exp: _____

Signature: _____

Send all orders to: Tyler Hicks, Prima Publishing and Communications
                      P.O. Box 12600 HC, Rocklin CA 95677

Or with Visa/MC, call orders at (916) 624-5718 Mon.–Fri. 9 AM–4 PM PST

INDEX